analytic
PROCESSES

for School Leaders

CYNTHIA T. RICHETTI AND BENJAMIN B. TREGOE

Association for Supervision and Curriculum Development
Alexandria, Virginia USA

Association for Supervision and Curriculum Development
1703 N. Beauregard St. • Alexandria, VA 22311-1714 USA
Telephone: 1-800-933-2723 or 703-578-9600 • Fax: 703-575-5400
Web site: http://www.ascd.org • E-mail: member@ascd.org

Printed in the United States of America.

ASCD Product No. 101017   s7/2001
ASCD member price: $18.95   nonmember price: $22.95

Library of Congress Cataloging-in-Publication Data
Richetti, Cynthia T.
    Analytic processes for school leaders / Cynthia T. Richetti and Benjamin B. Tregoe.
        p.   cm.
Includes bibliographical references and index.
    ISBN 0-87120-516-5 (alk. paper)
    1. School management and organization—Decision making.   2. Thought and thinking.
I. Tregoe, Benjamin B.   II. Title.
    LB2806 R5554 2001
    371.2—dc21   2001003270

07 06 05 04 03 02 01   10 9 8 7 6 5 4 3 2 1

Analytic Processes for School Leaders

List of Figures

Acknowledgments

This book is possible only because of the teachers, administrators, and students of the schools and school districts with whom we have been fortunate enough to work. We are most grateful to them. (See Appendix A for a listing.)

We are also indebted to Kepner-Tregoe, Inc., for their support and to those Kepner-Tregoe clients who made available an important member of their staff to work with a leadership team from a local middle school as part of the CompassQuest consortium, cosponsored by the Association for Supervision and Curriculum Development and the Tregoe Education Forum. (This project is described in Appendix B.) ASCD has been supportive of the work we are doing, and we are most appreciative.

We are also indebted to our colleagues at the Tregoe Education Forum, whose insights and suggestions have been invaluable—Bob Brock, Rick Fonte, Shari Johnson, Cass Love, Jim Sheerin, Amy Stempel, and especially, Bob Klempen and Mike Roche, with whom we have had the opportunity to work for the past eight years. And we would not be able to pursue our goals without those who have contributed financially and in other ways. We are grateful for their support.

Finally, we thank our editors, John O'Neil and Margaret Oosterman, for their many helpful suggestions, and Linda LePage and Carol Morello of Kepner-Tregoe, for their painstaking preparation of the manuscript.

Introduction

This book is about technology—but not the kind of technology you might expect. Billions of dollars are currently spent to educate, upgrade, introduce, and familiarize students and educators with the technology of our day. Usually, such efforts mean high technology, or computer-related information. Surely, this type of education is important, given the present and future state of the world.

We cannot help, however, but be struck by the fact that the same enthusiasm and investment do not exist for helping people enhance the natural technology with which they are born. We are witnessing incredible advancements within a lifetime (e.g., putting a man on the moon and mapping the human genome). The rate of change is simultaneously breathtaking and daunting. Yet human ingenuity and thinking are still at the heart of all this advancement.

Why do we seem to take for granted our ability to think? Why do we neglect to enhance the natural thinking and reasoning capabilities that are bestowed upon us? It seems almost as if we look to technology as a replacement for the need to think. Michael Bloomberg, founder of a multimedia conglomerate that relies heavily on delivering information through technology, asked recently, "Are we using technology as an excuse not to teach how to think and work with others? . . . Some think computer expertise is required for future success. I don't. Thinking and interpersonal communications skills have been, are, and will be keys to survival" (Bloomberg, 1997, pp. 153, 190).

As humans, we have the ability to reason through problems, challenges, and issues. We are not driven solely by instinct to react a certain way. We are capable of examination, reflection, and analysis—in short, thinking. And yet we often seem to treat thinking as if it were instinctive. Indeed, the capacity to think may be innate, but the ability to think *well* is an acquired skill. Rational thinking is the ability to accurately assess the various elements of a situation or challenge and use information effectively to form a sound conclusion.

When faced with problems, we typically need to respond or take some type of action. For many, taking action is not difficult. But how often is this action effective? How often do we look at decisions that others have made and wonder, "What were they thinking?" What we need is not a greater proclivity for action, but rather a greater incidence of rational action. Rational action is characterized by its appropriateness to meeting the needs of the situation, its effectiveness in resolving whatever was at issue, its ability to be used, and its support from key stakeholders.

Rational action requires rational thinking. Rational thinking doesn't happen by accident. How does one learn to develop effective solutions and take meaningful action to address life's challenges? If you're like most of us, you learned through experience, trial and error, and osmosis. Even if you consider yourself an effective problem solver, how much more effective might you be with some fine-tuning? How can you help others improve their abilities in this area?

A Better Process for Decision Making

In the late 1950s, Benjamin Tregoe and Charles Kepner, two research scientists working for the RAND Corporation, were conducting research with radar station crews for the Air Defense Command. They began to notice that certain air force officers in their study consistently made better decisions than others, even though all these officers had essentially the same training and experience and were presented with the same simulated air threats. Because the information the officers dealt with was the same, the difference in effectiveness had to lie in the process the decision makers used. Tregoe and Kepner theorized that the better decision makers followed a better process—that the process comprised a series of steps they followed to make their decisions and that the better decision makers were more aware of their decision-making process.

After they left RAND, Kepner and Tregoe continued their study of decision making. In 1958, they founded Kepner-Tregoe, Inc., now an international management consulting firm based in Princeton, New Jersey. Further research showed that better decision makers did indeed follow a better and more consistent process. Better decision makers were as unaware of their own process, however, as were the poor decision makers. Kepner and Tregoe conducted extensive research and ultimately identified and codified four analytic processes: decision analysis, potential problem analysis, problem analysis, and situation appraisal.

In the last 40 years, more than 20 million people have been trained in the Kepner-Tregoe®

problem-solving and decision-making processes. Today these processes are widely used, from the board room to the plant floor, in more than 1,400 of the world's most influential organizations, including Johnson & Johnson, Honda, IBM, NASA, Sony, and the World Bank. These decision-making strategies have been used in 44 countries and taught in 14 languages. The range of organizations and cultures, and the variety of issues to which these ideas have been applied, attest to their universality and broad applicability.

Bringing Critical-Thinking Skills to Education

In 1993, Tregoe founded the nonprofit Tregoe Education Forum to bring these same critical-thinking skills to elementary, middle, and high school students. The Tregoe Education Forum, under a license from Kepner-Tregoe, Inc., provides workshops and resource materials for teachers and administrators and enables them to provide K–12 students with the critical-thinking tools students need for personal development and success. The analytic processes have had a demonstrated effect, as reported by administrators and teachers, on elementary, middle, and high schools and their students in some 25 school districts across the country. Here are some reported benefits:

For students
• Better questioning techniques to gather, organize, and evaluate information.
• Increased ability to resolve real-life problems.

• Greater understanding of curriculum material.
• Improved ability to work in groups.

For teachers
• Increased student motivation and attention to lessons.
• More effective use of longer class periods.
• A proven way to integrate higher-order thinking skills into existing curriculum.

For administrators
• More effective resolution of critical school issues.
• Shared approach for handling complex issues and divergent opinions.

Purpose of the Book

The purpose of this book is to show educators how to apply the four rational-thinking approaches in an educational environment. It doesn't matter whether we are a 5th grade student, a superintendent of a major school district, or a special education teacher; if we need to make a decision, the basic tenets of effective decision making remain consistent. It is only the content of the decision that changes. Once we know the basic steps for effective issue resolution, we can apply those steps to almost any situation we face.

This book describes four step-by step approaches, or processes, for handling four common types of situations:

• When we need to make a choice.
• When we need to implement a change.
• When something goes wrong.
• When we need to better understand a complex issue.

When we break the thinking process down into steps, we reach better conclusions because we can understand, fine-tune, and improve our own approaches; communicate our rationale to others; more effectively involve others in solving problems; and transfer or teach these skills to others.

Each rational-thinking process is constructed of key process questions. The ability to ask effective questions is fundamental to the ability to solve problems. When we ask good questions, we can better involve others and use their best thinking, thus improving the quality of the outcome. Effective questioning transforms us and others from passive recipients of information to decision makers who proactively and effectively seek and use data.

In Chapter 1, we examine the need for rational thinking and process-based approaches for resolving issues. In Chapter 2, we look at the critical role that questioning plays in issue resolution. In Chapters 3 through 6, we examine in depth the four analytic processes. Each process helps us take a different type of action:

- *Decision analysis* helps us make choices.
- *Potential problem analysis* helps us implement changes or plans.
- *Problem analysis* helps us figure out why something has gone wrong.
- *Situation appraisal* helps us better understand and plan for resolution of a complex or confusing issue.

Although we examine each process individually—and each process can be used by itself—they are interrelated and are often used together. For example, suppose a school district is facing a teacher shortage. This is clearly a complex issue with many elements and ramifica-tions. The district might use situation appraisal to begin to examine this pressing issue. As situation appraisal is used to pinpoint and bring to the surface concerns related to the teacher shortage, several issues emerge. One issue might be that the district has been losing teachers to a neighboring district, thus exacerbating the shortage. Even though many theories are posited about why teachers are changing districts, nobody knows definitely what the reason is. Problem analysis can be used to help determine why the teachers are leaving. Once the cause is found, the district needs to make a choice about how to fix the problem. To make choices, decision analysis is helpful. After the district makes its choice, potential problem analysis helps ensure that the solution or choice is implemented well. The situation or issue and the goals of those responsible determine which process or processes to use. Finally, in Chapter 7, we look at simple ways to get started using the four analytic tools, including how to decide which tools to use for different situations.

New Trends in Education

Today, several trends mark the educational landscape. Administrative trends include the move to decentralization and site-based management. Serious efforts involve changing the locus of authority and accountability. Principals and others may have authority over much larger budgets. Issues that previously may have been elevated to higher district levels for resolution must now be handled closer to where the issues originate. How do people recognize which issues must be dealt with? How do they effectively involve increasingly diverse and demanding stakeholders? How do they avoid the problems that change can bring? How do they evaluate the success of their efforts? New responsibilities require new skills.

In the classroom, we see continued trends toward engaging instruction and authentic assessment. The rational-thinking approaches draw students into learning by encouraging them to form and ask good questions. Their input is necessary and valued. Because the analytic tools help make their students' thinking visible, teachers find it easier to understand, coach, and assess student thinking in given situations. Other movements deal with the need to prepare students to handle life issues outside the classroom: life skills, career counseling, values and ethics, and prevention of substance abuse. The analytic tools described in this book are rooted in teaching the skills we all need to better understand and address the issues we face in life. By learning process-based approaches to situations, students gain skills that will serve them throughout life—in and outside of school.

We hope you are intrigued by what you read in the following chapters. We hope that we have managed to make a case for the value of rational thinking. We are awed by the power of the natural computer with which we all were born. We encourage you to imagine what would be possible—in our own lives, in our schools, and in our communities—if we all paused to think first, before we take rational action!

Rational Thinking as a Process

Solutions to significant problems facing modern society demand a widespread qualitative improvement in thinking and understanding. . . . We need a breakthrough in the *quality* of thinking employed by both decision makers and by each of us in our daily affairs. [emphasis in original]

—ORNSTEIN, IN COSTA, 1991

The assertion that society and individuals can benefit from improving the ways we approach and consider some of life's toughest problems is hard to argue with. The news media are rife with examples of questionable responses or solutions to situations and events. We all, average citizens to world leaders, struggle to develop creative, workable solutions to pressing problems and issues. Statistics abound on studies that have demonstrated students' ability to memorize facts but not apply them. Parents wrestle with helping their children successfully navigate in an increasingly complicated world.

A lack of thought does not characterize most of these scenarios, but rather an incomplete consideration of the situation. Typically, poor decisions or other mistakes are a result of flawed or incomplete thinking, not the absence of thinking.

This book is about rational thinking. The phrase is not a redundancy. Contrary to popular opinion, not all thinking is rational, at least as we would define rational. Rational thinking is the ability to consider the relevant variables of a

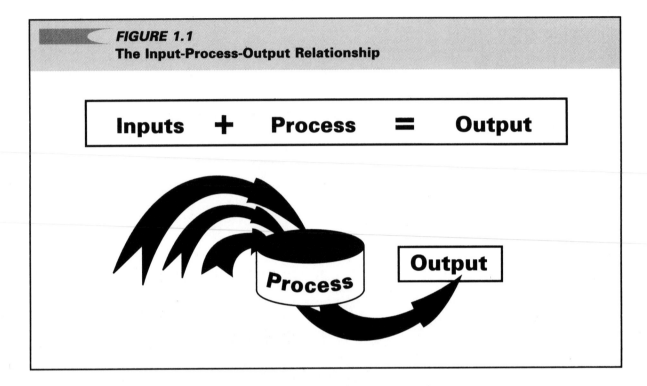

FIGURE 1.1
The Input-Process-Output Relationship

Inputs + Process = Output

Process

Output

situation and to access, organize, and analyze relevant information (e.g., facts, opinions, judgments, and data) to arrive at a sound conclusion.

Indeed, several authors have defined intelligence, at least in part, as the ability to solve problems. For example, Sternberg (1996) writes:

> Successful intelligence as I view it involves analytical, creative, and practical aspects. The analytic aspect is used to solve problems, the creative aspect to decide what problems to solve, and the practical aspect to make solutions effective. (p. 47)

Although the study of thought and thinking as an end in itself is a worthwhile pursuit, our focus is on the need to *apply* thought (i.e., use thought as a precursor to action). Rational thinking helps us arrive at a conclusion to be able to *do* something (i.e., take rational action).

Rational Thinking as a Series of Steps

Much of what we do in everyday life involves a process—a series of actionable, repeatable steps that can be performed to accomplish a desired goal. For example, we have a process for baking a cake, writing an expository essay, and changing a tire. A process is a meaningful, repeatable series of steps that produces an outcome. Every *process* requires *inputs* to produce some *output*. Figure 1.1 shows the connection among these three elements.

Let's consider that we are making barbecued ribs. To make delicious barbecued ribs (output), we need fresh meat, a tasty sauce, and other ingredients (inputs). We also need to ensure that the grilling (process) is good. We can have the best-tasting sauce in the world, but if we let the ribs burn, we're not going to have tasty ribs.

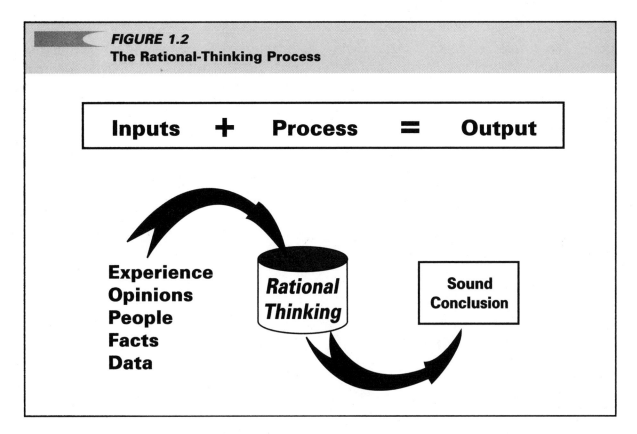

FIGURE 1.2
The Rational-Thinking Process

Inputs + Process = Output

Experience
Opinions
People
Facts
Data

Rational Thinking

Sound Conclusion

Let's now look at the rational-thinking process. In arriving at a conclusion, we must take a series of inputs and do something to them (a process). Figure 1.2 shows how the input-process-output model for rational thinking might look.

The same logic that applies to the ribs applies to the rational-thinking process. A sound conclusion (output) requires high-quality inputs (e.g., accurate information and access to the right people) and a high-quality thinking process. Focusing on the inputs is not enough to ensure success; we need to give equal attention to the process or what we do with the inputs—how we collect, organize, and analyze them.

Let's look at a specific situation where rational thinking applies. A group of student-athletes has been asked to recommend a dis-

trictwide substance abuse policy for all student athletes. The output for this situation would be the substance abuse policy. What would the inputs be? They might be statistics on substance abuse by student athletes or opinions from students, coaches, administrators, parents, and board members on what should be done. Maybe the inputs would include examples from other districts' substance abuse policies. As with most complex situations, some ideas and opinions might conflict. How do the students get from juggling all these inputs to developing a sound student-athlete substance abuse policy?

The process of rational thinking is needed. But where did we learn to think rationally? Most people can't cite a specific way they learned. Typically, they learn through osmosis or experience. If you ask most people what steps they go through while thinking, they are unable to articulate them. Consequently, they are unable to critique their own thinking process—and unable to teach others. Myers (1986) uses an analogy to show this difficulty:

> When we see a juggler effortlessly tossing oranges in the air, we fail to appreciate the first stumbling efforts and the hours of practice that laid the groundwork for that proficiency. The same holds true for expert critical thinkers. All experts started as novices—struggling with basic concepts, questions, and issues—as they developed the thought processes that would help them make sense of things. The problem is that by the time they have achieved their expertise, many of those thought processes have become so automatic, internalized, and implicit that the experts have difficulty explaining explicitly how they think. (p. 16)

Costs of an Invisible Process

Imagine learning to drive without guidance. What if you didn't know what constituted good driving? What if you had no model for how to drive, how to start a car, how to put the car in gear, and how and when to brake? How many of you would put your 16-year-old behind the wheel without providing any driving instruction, either formally or informally? Yet a similar situation occurs when our children are expected to think rationally. Furthermore, who taught us the basics of rational thinking? Where did we learn to arrive at sound conclusions? How will our children learn?

The main reason that rational thinking is not addressed in the same way as learning to drive, write, or play a sport is that it has been treated primarily as an invisible process. It hasn't been regarded as something that can be broken down into a series of actionable steps. The focus in a thinking situation is typically on gathering the inputs—information, data, and opinions—not on how to organize and analyze them. Consequently, rational thinking has been an invisible process. People arrive at conclusions, but they don't know too much about how they get there. What are the unintended but real consequences of allowing thinking to be an invisible process? Here are a few:

• We are forced to learn about thinking through trial and error—an inefficient and often costly way to learn. Without an understanding of what constitutes good thinking, we cannot proactively critique and improve own thinking. We are forced to assess our success after the fact.

• We are limited in our ability to teach others to think rationally. If we do not clearly understand the process of thinking, how can we help others improve their thinking? What do we teach? Beyer (1984) addresses this concern:

> A second obstacle to effective teaching and learning of thinking skills lies in our failure to identify with precision those cognitive operations that constitute the individual skills we choose to teach. . . . If we knew the essential components of these thinking skills, we could devise better ways to teach these skills to students. (p. 487)

• When we don't have a conscious process to follow, we view every situation that involves new information or events as different, thus requiring a new approach. Little knowledge is transferred from one situation to the next, leading us to overrely on experience, which may or may not be relevant to a new situation.

• Working with others may be chaotic and difficult in the absence of a common approach. Everyone tends to approach a situation from a slightly or vastly different angle. Imagine someone learning to drive in a carful of people who all drive differently and are all coaching the driver to do different things.

• We overrely on content. That content is an essential and important part of rational thinking is unquestionable. After all, a conclusion requires some consideration of content. Often, we may have the information needed, but we use it ineffectively. We overlook or minimize vital pieces of information or place too much emphasis on relatively unimportant or irrelevant pieces of information (Kepner & Tregoe, 1965). Our process, not our content, is faulty.

Different Strategies for Different Situations

Different situations require different types of thinking. Taken at face value, this rationale makes sense. Yet most problem-solving tools tend to treat all problem situations the same. Such tools are some variation on the following approach: Identify the problem, gather information, brainstorm possible solutions, select the best solution, and implement it. Treating all problem situations with the same approach, however, is akin to a doctor treating all complaints with aspirin. If you have a headache, aspirin may help. If you have nausea or difficulty breathing, however, you will probably require a

different treatment. Beyer (1984) sees a similar approach in education:

> We sometimes use labels with different meanings to stand for a single skill. For instance, many educators equate problem solving with decision making, and many others also equate reflective thinking with either or both of these—despite the fact that each phrase describes a particular set of subskills that are used in a unique order to accomplish a different kind of task. . . . Clearing up the ambiguities regarding which thinking skills to teach and how we define each is an important first step toward improving the thinking skills of students. (p. 487)

Investigating a situation that has already happened to determine why something went wrong requires a different approach from looking into the future to anticipate future problems. Figure 1.3 (p. 12) identifies four types of situations, each requiring a different thinking approach.

We offer four analytic processes, designed to address the unique requirements of each type of situation and to produce a high-quality conclusion. These processes are presented briefly here and discussed in detail in subsequent chapters. The four processes are decision analysis (see Chapter 3), potential problem analysis (see Chapter 4), problem analysis (see Chapter 5), and situation appraisal (see Chapter 6).

Decision Analysis

This analytic process addresses the basic question, Which one should we choose? It helps us, as decision makers, establish a clear set of criteria with which to evaluate possible choices or courses of action. Those criteria are then used

---

> ![gray bar] **FIGURE 1.3**
> **Four Types of Situations**

Situation	Definition
Decision	One course of action or solution must be selected from among several possible options.
Implementation	Upcoming plans, changes, and actions will be implemented.
Problem	Something has gone wrong or an unknown cause has produced some undesired effect.
Complex	There are multifaceted scenarios having multiple variables and elements.

---

to identify what choice or course of action best meets the goals for a particular decision. Before we make a choice, however, we must consider the risks associated with an option. Decision analysis helps guard against the tendency to immediately start evaluating options without having a clear idea or consensus on specific goals or objectives. School-related examples of when decision analysis might apply include the following:

- Selecting a new scheduling system.
- Hiring a new assistant principal.
- Deciding how to reconfigure some classes to handle increased or decreased enrollment.

Potential Problem Analysis

This tool examines the question, What lies ahead? (e.g., What could go wrong?). It helps ensure the success of upcoming events, plans, or changes by asking us to identify problems that might arise and actions we might take to prevent them. In addition, we identify actions to take should problems arise anyway. Thus, we can be better prepared for future trouble either

by eliminating problems or minimizing their effect. This process helps combat the human tendency to be reactive—by not worrying about something until it happens. School-related examples of when potential problem analysis might apply are these:

- Hosting an important function (e.g., a science competition or inservice day).
- Implementing a new policy or procedure.
- Preparing for an upcoming accreditation review.

Problem Analysis

This tool examines cause-and-effect relationships in a search for the true cause. Problem analysis helps us answer the question, Why did this happen? as we first collect and organize data relevant to a problem. Then we develop and test possible causes against these data to see if the causes make sense. Testing helps us narrow our search systematically. Often, when something goes wrong, we typically point fingers and fix blame. Problem analysis encourages us to clearly understand a problem before we jump to misinformed conclusions and waste time, money, and energy on solutions that won't work. Here are school-related examples of when problem analysis might be used:

• Determining why scores have fallen at a given school.
• Figuring out the reason for an unexplained increase in teacher absenteeism.
• Examining declining student enrollment.

Situation Appraisal

This process addresses the basic question, What's going on? It helps us sort through multiple issues, clarify meaning to ensure common understanding, set priorities, and plan next steps. Complex issues usually involve multiple concerns, viewpoints, and tangents. Emotions are often involved, and stakeholders all seem to have different agendas. When we deal with complicated issues, especially emotional ones, we often lump them into general categories and then label those categories (e.g., student achievement or staff morale).

Situation appraisal guards against the tendency to generalize when we need specifics to reach a common understanding and take effective action. School-related examples of when situation appraisal might be used are these:

• Handling a conflict over something that has happened (e.g., a discipline issue).
• Airing concerns of key stakeholders on a particular issue (e.g., school safety).
• Preparing for a major new initiative (e.g., new standards).

Figure 1.4 (p. 14) shows how the four analytic processes match the four types of situations. To address a given situation, a specific type of response or rational action is needed. As the figure shows, each analytic process consists of a series of steps that describe the approach to the situation. The processes help us form sound conclusions and prepare to take rational action. An acronym for each process—SELECT, PLAN, FIND, and SCAN—helps us remember the steps and the overall purpose.

Benefits of Treating Rational Thinking as a Process

If we treat rational thinking as a process—a series of definable, actionable, repeatable steps that produce a meaningful conclusion—we can derive many benefits. Here are some of them:

• *Make thinking visible.* Unless we know how someone arrived at a conclusion, we can critique only the answer or conclusion. If we break the process of thinking into individual steps and make it visible, we are better able to critique both our own thinking process and that of others. Math teachers often advise their students to show their work. If all that counts is the answer, the work (or process) is irrelevant. Showing the work allows teachers (and students) to know just where the students may have gone wrong. Did they totally miss a concept or did they make a simple transposition error? Where in the process or to what concepts must students pay extra attention? Do the students' errors show where reteaching may be required?
• *Help in learning a new skill.* An example of learning a new skill might be learning to serve a tennis ball. When coaches teach someone how to serve, they typically break the process down into a series of steps that address elements such as positioning the feet, tossing the ball, and

FIGURE 1.4
Types of Situations and Corresponding Analytic Processes

Situation	Definition	What's Needed as a Basis for Rational Action	Analytic Process
Decision	One course of action or solution must be selected from among several possible options.	Select the best possible option after evaluating options against criteria and then considering risks.	**Decision Analysis** State the decision. Establish and classify objectives. List alternatives. Evaluate alternatives. Consider risks. Trust your work—pick a winner!
Implementation	Upcoming plans, changes, and actions will be implemented.	Identify actions needed for successful implementation after identifying potential problems and how to handle them.	**Potential Problem Analysis** Predict potential problems. List likely causes. Agree on preventive actions. Note contingent actions.
Problem	Something has gone wrong or an unknown cause has produced some undesired effect.	Analyze relevant data to evaluate possible causes and determine the true cause.	**Problem Analysis** Focus on the problem. Identify what *is* and *is not*. Narrow possible causes. Determine the true cause.
Complex	There are multi-faceted scenarios having multiple variables and elements.	Understand relevant variables, their priorities, and possible action plans.	**Situation Appraisal** See the issues. Clarify the issues. Assess priorities. Name next steps.

Source: Adapted from Richetti & Sheerin, 1999, p. 60.

moving the racket. Each of these skills can be examined and practiced independent of the others, then in combination. When each element is correctly applied in concert with the others, the process of serving a tennis ball is complete. The same process holds true for thinking. As in learning a skill, we can break problem solving into individual steps that we practice. We can thus improve our own thinking—and help others improve theirs.

• *Lessen our reliance on experience or "gut feel."* Experience can be a powerful teacher, but in a rapidly changing world, it has its limits. What we already know becomes outdated too quickly for us to rely on knowledge or experience alone.

Often we think we have seen a particular situation before, and thus we might come to a similar conclusion. But closer examination may reveal more differences between situations than we had originally realized. Old solutions don't always apply to new situations. Studies have shown that little correlation exists between someone's certainty about the correctness of a difficult answer and that answer being right (Perkins, 1981). In the absence of a more compelling way to reach conclusions, we sometimes revert to "gut feel." People are often required to work together in finding a solution or reaching a conclusion. Not everyone, however, has had the same experiences. The steps in the process of rational thinking help us sort out different opinions and consider relevant variables and information.

• *Apply the process in new or unfamiliar situations.* If we have a process for thinking, we are able to successfully repeat that process in other situations. If we are unaware of what we do or how we do it, we are less likely to replicate our successes. But if we are aware of a process for rational thinking, we can maximize our chances for success by consciously making required adjustments and always considering successful thinking's key ingredients.

Because the process of rational thinking remains the same—independent of the content a situation requires—we can apply the process to any situation, *even though the content of the situation may be totally different or new to us.* Rational thinking allows us to make decisions in new or unfamiliar situations by providing steps that help us gather and process relevant information.

• *Help others improve their thinking abilities.* When we regard thinking as a process, we can teach others how to improve their own rational thinking. Good thinking used to be seen almost as an innate quality; people were either good

decision makers or they weren't. Now we know differently. We can help people improve their ability to think through situations by teaching them a process. In the way baseball players improve their batting averages by working on their swing, practicing hitting various pitches, and conditioning, we can help others improve their thinking by coaching them in the steps required for rational thinking.

Working and Thinking with Others

Framing rational thinking as a process has other benefits. One such benefit becomes evident when people are required to work together in a problem situation. As educators, we are rarely faced with a problem for which we alone have all the necessary information and answers. We must usually work with others, whether we are dealing with a disciplinary issue, addressing a community crisis, or making curricular decisions. Students, too, must work with others on issues and problems, both in and out of class (e.g., completing a team assignment, organizing a bake sale, choosing a theme for the prom, or helping a friend). As students enter the work force, they need to know how to work with others to resolve problems and address issues.

Even if a situation or circumstance does not mandate involving others, we know there are important reasons to include other people. First, effectively involving others typically increases the quality of the output or conclusion that is reached (Perkins, 1981). If we solicit others' input, ideas, and critique, we usually produce an end result that is better than if we work alone. Second, we typically create more commitment to the solution (Vroom & Yetton, 1973). This commitment is especially important

15

when the success of implementation depends on others. In a school environment, a decision is rarely made that does not affect others. When we effectively involve others in solving the problem, we increase their acceptance of the solution and their willingness to implement it.

A visible thinking process provides guidelines to people who must work together on an issue. It functions much the same as the rules of a game. Once you know the rules of soccer, you can play soccer with anyone else who knows the rules. You don't have to focus on what the rules are; you can focus on working with your teammates to win the game. Once group members agree on the process or approach they use to handle a situation, they can focus on what the solution should be. A visible rational process allows people to concentrate on developing the best possible resolution to a problem without getting mired down and arguing with others about *how* to do it.

Expectations within and outside school often change, and people of different backgrounds and areas of expertise are required to work together. As we discussed earlier, people tend to rely on their content expertise and experience. But this approach is problematic when different areas of expertise or content knowledge are represented. We can use a rational-thinking process to help us accommodate different content and experiences. When a process provides a road map or framework for approaching a problem, different viewpoints can lead to healthy discussion and debate rather than to increasing polarization of group members.

People may acknowledge the value of involving others in decision making and problem solving, but they shy away from that involvement because they are afraid of the potential conflict or emotion. A rational-thinking process

helps us channel that emotion and use it more effectively. Using a process prevents discussions from careening off into the stratosphere, never again to return to the point or topic at hand, and allows group members to know exactly where they are—what they have accomplished, what they are working on, and what they should do next. A process accommodates a variety of viewpoints and emotions. Once people know they have been heard, they are more ready to listen to others.

The rational process approach also applies to cooperative learning. Many teachers tell us they are reluctant to use cooperative learning techniques because such techniques make it difficult to keep students on task and to know where students stand. Using a process approach in group problem-solving situations helps teachers—and students—quickly assess where they are and where they need to go.

How These Tools Can Help Students

We have talked primarily about how these tools (decision analysis, potential problem analysis, problem analysis, and situation analysis) may be used to handle issues that schools and districts face. The tools are equally applicable to situations that students face. The content of the situations may differ, but a student who needs to choose what elective to take or how to help a friend in trouble can benefit from approaching the situation thoughtfully and logically.

Applying these analytic tools in the curriculum helps students not only learn the tools, but also better understand the material. If we use decision analysis to examine a decision that has already been made, we can better understand the considerations of the decision makers and the issues they had to weigh. For example, if we use decision analysis to explore Thomas Jefferson's decision to support the Louisiana Purchase, we understand more clearly the factors he had to weigh, the oppositions he faced, and the risks he took. Several studies demonstrate that deeper understanding of curriculum material (e.g., comprehension beyond recall) increases retention (Langer, 1997). The more heavily students rely on recall of material, the more quickly they forget the material, and the less able they are to apply it or extrapolate from it.

Richard Paul (1990) relates a story about John Dewey that illustrates the difference between recall and understanding. Dewey visits a class and asks the students what they would find if they dug a hole in the earth and kept on digging. Getting no response, he repeats the question; again, he faces nothing but silence.

The teacher chides Dr. Dewey, "You're asking the wrong question."

Turning to the class, she asks, "What is the state of the center of the earth?"

The class replies in unison, "Igneous fusion."

This example shows that the students were able to recall the answer as long as the question was asked in a specific way. If the students had understood the concept, they would have been able to apply that knowledge by answering Dr. Dewey's question.

We know that involvement increases retention and builds meaning for students (Goodlad, 1984). For the Louisiana Purchase example, when students think through the variables and reach a conclusion using the four analytic tools, they experience the dilemmas of a situation more actively and deeply than when they simply remember the reasons Jefferson made the Louisiana Purchase.

Other studies show that understanding and retention increase when people consider information or issues from multiple perspectives. The tools provide a framework to help them examine issues from more than one viewpoint.

Several researchers and educators have pointed out that most real issues needing resolution have multiple components and several possible solutions, not one correct answer. These ill-structured problems vary considerably from the well-defined and well-structured problems students often face in class (King & Kitchener, 1994; Paul, 1990). The four analytic processes provide an approach to addressing ill-structured problems.

Finally, we need to consider the applicability of what students learn in class to life outside class. Students are not always clear about how they will apply the content they've learned. How they learn to think about that content—the process they develop—is a skill they can transfer to any content and apply to life. The aim of rational thinking is to teach them to think so they can arrive at meaningful conclusions. Wales, Nardi, and Stager (1986) believe that decision making is a key component in the process:

Decision making gives thinking a purpose. Through our decisions, which are based on what we have learned both in and out of school, we determine the course of our lives. We make decisions that affect both our success as workers and our success as people. Since this is the promise of education, it seems clear that the new paradigm should be: schooling focused on decision making, the thinking skills that serve it, and the knowledge base that supports it. (p. 38)

Students can use these strategies not only to analyze decisions and issues from curriculum material, but also to address other types of issues they face outside class:

- Helping a friend suspected of being suicidal.
- Choosing a career to investigate.
- Assessing situations involving substance abuse and violence.
- Preparing to attend a new school.
- Developing better study habits.

The four analytic tools—decision analysis, potential problem analysis, problem analysis, and situation appraisal—can help students in a number of ways:

- Encourage them to consider more deeply complex issues or ideas.
- Support them as they develop sound conclusions that consider relevant variables and information.
- Provide them with a road map for guiding group work.
- Involve them as they examine issues from several perspectives.
- Provide approaches they can apply in other classes and on other curriculum material.

- Help them gather, organize, and analyze relevant information.
- Establish a basis from which they are able to diagnose, assess, and improve their own thinking processes.
- Provide a framework from which they can present and justify conclusions.
- Provide strategies to help them better handle real-life issues and problems.

Once we see rational thinking as a process, we can see how to improve our own or others' thinking. We can also more easily envision how rational thinking can be taught and applied meaningfully. When we identify the four different types of situations, each of which requires a different thinking strategy, we ensure that we use the best tool for the job.

As we have seen, each analytic process is designed to help answer a different overarching question. Each process consists of a series of questions organized to achieve the desired end result. The ability to form and ask good questions is fundamental to our analytic processes. Because of the connection between rational thinking and effective questioning, we examine the need for questioning in the next chapter.

Thinking About Questions

Questions are the important thing,
answers are less important. Learning to ask a
good question is the heart of intelligence. . . .
Questions are for thinkers.

—SCHANK, 1991

Weach of the four thinking processes we examine in depth comprises a series of sequenced questions. These questions help identify, solicit, organize, and analyze the information vital to effective problem solving.

Much has been written about the importance of questioning. In this chapter, we examine some reasons questioning has been, and continues to be, important. We focus on why questioning is critical for effective issue resolution. For example, as we successfully address any issue, questioning allows us to do the following:

When it comes to handling life's issues, we all need to be thinkers. And to be good thinkers, we need to ask good questions. Whether we are students, teachers, administrators, or parents, being a skilled questioner is fundamental to resolving issues effectively. Answers matter, but without questions, there are no answers. If we can ask the right questions, we can always find the right answers.

• Clarify and frame messy or ill-structured problems.
• Identify and gather missing information.
• Sort through available information and arrive at conclusions.

- Better understand the needs and beliefs of stakeholders.
- Solicit others' opinions and analyses of a situation.
- Increase commitment to a solution by raising the quality of that solution and involving others in the decision-making process.

Why Learning to Question Is Increasingly Important

We are part of a revolution in information technology. Through computers, the Internet, media, and other communications technology, we have ready access to more information than ever before. That information changes rapidly and quickly becomes obsolete; it is estimated that half of what an engineering graduate learns is obsolete within four years (Rubenstein, 1998).

Access to information increases, and the information changes more rapidly than our ability to acquire or master it. Gone are the days when we could be content masters or gurus. The real gurus now are the people who know how to sort through, assess, and *use* relevant information. According to Patricia Vail, "The educated person used to be the one who could find information. Now, with a flood of data available, the educated mind is not the one that can master the facts, but the one able to ask the 'winnowing question'" (Vail, in Healy, 1990, p. 338).

This information explosion, and the rapid obsolescence of information it helps create, require us to become lifelong learners. Taking charge of our own learning means that we should ask questions to determine what we need to learn and to obtain and digest the necessary information. In today's world, we cannot be pas-

sive learners who rely on others to tell us what we need to know. According to Postman and Weingarten (1969), learning to ask questions is the key:

> Once you have learned how to ask questions—relevant and appropriate and substantial questions—you have learned how to learn and no one can keep you from learning whatever you want or need to know. (p. 23)

As changes occur in the workplace and in the education arena, we are expected to work effectively with a wider range of people. Experts from a variety of disciplines and backgrounds must increasingly work together to resolve the issues that face their school, district, and organization.

When Teachers Ask the Questions

According to Degarmo (in Wilen, 1991), good questioning means good teaching:

> To question well is to teach well. In the skillful use of the question more than anything else lies the fine art of teaching; for in it we have the guide to clear and vivid ideas, the quick spur to imagination, the stimulus to thought, the incentive to action. (p. 5)

Most of the current focus on teaching looks at questioning as either a primary teaching vehicle (e.g., Socratic questioning) or as an additional tool to support, extend, or reinforce teaching. Asking questions is one way to engage learners in the learning process. Questions can encourage deeper thought and investigation, and they can serve as a jumping-off point for further study. We know that the more learners are involved in the material, the more they understand and the longer they retain that understanding (Goodlad, 1984).

Let's look at what else is known about the use of questioning in the classroom. Wilen (1991) conducted a review of research about questioning practices in the classroom. Among his findings were the following:

• Studies show that, in general, a positive correlation exists between frequency of questioning and increased student learning. One study shows that a 5 percent increase in higher-order questions posed by teachers resulted in a 40 percent increase in the quality and depth of student answers. Other studies show mixed results and little correlation between higher-order questions and the quality of the answers.

• Elementary teachers said they use questions in the classroom mainly to assess the effectiveness of their teaching, diagnose areas of difficulty, and check recall. The survey results suggest that teachers see questions primarily as vehicles to assess what the students know and how well they have been taught—not to stretch students' thinking or force them to think in new ways.

• Teachers ask 300 to 400 questions daily. Elementary teachers tend to ask more questions than junior high teachers. Experienced senior high teachers tend to ask more questions than inexperienced teachers.

• Another study of 6th grade history teachers found that 77 percent of teacher questions were factual (i.e., required factual answers). Only 17 percent of teacher questions required students to do more than recall facts. Studies of junior high and gifted students found that most questions require simple memorization to answer. A study of high school social studies students found that more questions were asked at the memory level than all other types of questions combined.

Goodlad (1984), in his landmark study of schools, assessed how students and teachers spent their time in class. He found these facts:

• An average of 75 percent of class time was spent on instruction.
• Of this instructional time, 70 percent was oral—primarily teacher-dominated talk. Teachers outtalked their students by a ratio of 3 to 1.
• Ninety-five percent of this teacher talk was instruction through telling; no response was required from the students. Students were required to reason, provide opinions, share thoughts, and so forth less than 1 percent of the time.

Cecil (1995) discusses a 1992 study by Bromley, which confirms the predominance of factual questions in the classroom: 75 percent of the questions teachers asked were factual. In 30 minutes of observation, teachers asked, on average, 70 factual questions. Factual questions predominated in a review of written material as well. In basal readers, 50 percent of the questions were factual. (The study can be found in Bromley, 1992.)

Even though the need to understand certain facts and information is clear, an overreliance on factual questions has a price: It encourages passive learning, rewards short-term memory over the ability to synthesize information, discourages creativity, and reinforces in children the belief that facts are more important than their own thoughts or evaluations of ideas (Cecil, 1995). One study shows a specific condition that produced a positive correlation between the questions students were asked and the answers they gave: When students were taught to recognize the type of question asked, the quality of their answers improved (Kyzer, 1996).

Why would teachers place such reliance on these lower-order questions? Some suggested reasons are that such questions allow students to give quick and concise answers (Cecil, 1995), and they allow the teacher to control the pace and atmosphere and avoid the uncertainty of messy answers (Eales-White, 1998). Because there are "right" answers for these types of questions, teachers don't have to deal with the uncertainty that open-ended and higher-order questions tend to encourage. They can quickly assess the accuracy of the answer and move on or reteach. Another reason teachers rely on lower-order questions is that they have seen this type of question modeled. Without further skill development, teachers tend to teach the way they were taught. Our curricula also tend to be fact oriented, not thought oriented (Johnson, 1992). It thus stands to reason that recitation of facts is what we test for and reward.

Researchers who compared U.S. teachers to Japanese teachers found that "they ask questions for different reasons in the United States and Japan. In the United States, teachers ask questions to get answers, but in Japan, teachers pose questions to stimulate thought. In fact, they consider questions to be poor if they elicit immediate answers because this indicates that students were not challenged to think" (Berryman & Bailey, 1992, p. 58). These findings were

further reinforced in an article (Olson, 1999) examining a well-known study involving videotaped classrooms in three countries. The article describes a study by Stigler and Hiebert, who analyzed videotaped classrooms in the United States, Japan, and Germany. In Japan, effective instruction was seen as that which forced students to stretch. If students wrestled with a concept, they were required to think. This approach was seen as an effective lesson. In the United States, most teachers provided the concepts to students. If students struggled at all with the concepts, the U.S. teachers would immediately "retreat and repeat" the lesson. (The study can be found in Stigler & Hiebert, 1999.)

When we review the literature on questioning, it is clear that, to date, the majority of attention has gone to teacher questioning. Actual classroom practice reflects the reality of this emphasis. Cecil (1995) found that for every question a student asked, teachers asked 27 questions. Other studies verify these findings in elementary through secondary school classrooms. One study found an average of 84 teacher-generated questions during a class hour and two student-generated questions. Over the course of a school year, this practice translates into each pupil asking one question each month (Dillon, 1990).

When Students Ask the Questions

Let's look at some reasons for students to develop their own questions:

• *Increases motivation to learn.* Learners of all ages are motivated to learn the answers to questions, especially when they play a role in framing the questions. Learning immediately becomes more relevant to the learner, and relevance increases the learner's desire to know. "Understanding is question driven. To understand we must be able to ask questions, to wonder about things we are reading or hearing about" (Schank, 1991, p. 209).

• *Improves comprehension and retention.* Students comprehend and retain more when they construct their own questions (Cecil, 1995). Not only are students more motivated to learn, they are also more likely to learn when they form and investigate the answers to questions they have developed. One technique that distinguishes competent readers and thinkers is that they are able to generate and consider questions about the text (Cecil, 1995).

• *Encourages creativity and innovation.* We have already mentioned that answering factual questions engenders passivity. To further our thinking and see things in new ways, we need to be able to ask new questions. Posing and investigating questions drive our creativity (Schank, 1991). Vail notes, "By engaging students only in a quest for the correct answer, rather than for the interesting question, we condemn them to live inside other men's discoveries" (Vail, in Healy, 1990, p. 295).

• *Teaches how to think and learn.* Earlier in the chapter, we talked about the importance of developing skills for lifelong learning. Learning how to ask questions helps students take charge of their own learning and thinking both in and out of school. Depending on others to generate the questions breeds dependence on others for our own learning and growth. According to Beyer (1987),

> Using teacher-asked questions as the major device for guiding students in the use of thinking skills contradicts a major

goal of the teaching of thinking—making students dependent on someone else to initiate and direct thinking. An active thinking student ought to be able to generate and direct his or her own thinking. Learning how to invent one's own question enables students to achieve this goal. (p. 154)

• *Provides a basis for problem solving and decision making.* Asking effective questions is basic to solving problems. If we are not able to ask good questions, we cannot obtain or analyze information that will enable us to arrive at sound conclusions. Without questions, we are forever dependent on the information and conclusions of others. The greater our ability to ask good questions, the more we can take charge of our own problem solving and help others with theirs.

What Constitutes Good Problem-Solving Questioning?

Imagine a situation in which a student asks a teacher for help choosing a topic for a science project. Let's look at two possible ways the conversation might unfold, then examine the kinds of questions used in the two scenarios.

Conversation A

Teacher: Have you thought about photosynthesis? You seemed to be really interested in plants, and I don't believe anyone else is doing something in this area.

Student: You're right. I love gardening and working in the greenhouse. But I also love animals. I have several pets at home.

Teacher: I didn't realize that. Of course, several students already have chosen projects involving

23

pets. Don't forget that there are limited library resources, so the more projects there are on a given subject, the fewer books will be available. Are you interested in endangered species of animals?

Student: I guess so, but I like finding out more about my own animals.

Teacher: What about a project that combines plants and animals? Like maybe looking at the nutritive value of plant matter in dog food?

Student: It seems so chemical oriented. I like playing with my animals.

Teacher: Let's try to think of another interesting plant topic. How about comparing the hardiness of different strains of tomatoes—or comparing the effectiveness of various organic pest controls?

Conversation B

Teacher: What are some things you are interested in and why do they appeal to you?

Student: Well, I like gardening because I get a lot of satisfaction from taking care of something and seeing it grow. There is no feeling like eating a carrot you've grown from seed. I guess that is partly why I also love spending time with my pets. It feels good to take good care of them. And I like teaching them new things. Did you know that I show my dog in obedience classes?

Teacher: I had no idea. It sounds like you have a pretty clear understanding of some possible areas of interest. What else do you think you might want to consider in choosing a topic?

Student: Well, I have had trouble checking out books from the library when too many people are working on similar things. So, I guess I'd like to choose something that was a little different. Also, I need to choose something I can work on at home or through the Internet. It's hard for me to get rides anywhere. I'd really like to do something with my dogs.

Teacher: What topics would allow you to work with your dogs, work at home, and also be somewhat unusual?

Student: I don't know. How about something with dog training—like using dogs for search and rescue or to help physically challenged people? Or I've heard something about pets being able to predict earthquakes and things like that. I've also heard about intelligence tests for dogs.

Teacher: Those all sound like intriguing projects. What's a next step?

Student: I'll think about it over the weekend and give you something on Monday if that's okay. Thanks a lot for your help. You've given me some great ideas!

Examining the Conversations

Consider the two conversations as you read these questions:

- Which conversation requires the student to think more?
- In which conversation do we learn more about the student's interests and considerations?
- After which conversation is it most likely the student will feel ownership over the solution (topic chosen)?

FIGURE 2.1
Comparison of Process and Content Questions

Process Questions	Content Questions
Tend to be open-ended.	Tend to be closed-ended.
Apply to any situation.	Apply to a specific situation.
Generate much information from few questions.	Generate little information from many questions.
Put burden of knowing content on answerer.	Put burden of knowing content on questioner.
Systematically probe for information gaps.	Randomly find information gaps.
Develop thinking skills of answerer.	Produce limited developmental benefit.

• In which conversation are questions asked that are most easily transferable to other decision-making situations?

If you answered Conversation B to all the questions, we agree. What do you notice about Conversation A? Do you notice how hard the teacher has to work? Even though it is the student's project, the teacher is valiantly trying to generate ideas and help. The teacher in Conversation B used *process* questions, while the teacher in Conversation A used *content* questions. Figure 2.1 compares process and content questions.

Even though the figure shows the value of process questions, we know that teachers tend to ask content questions—those that require recall or recitation of information. We have discussed evidence of this finding, which comes from studies that identify the kinds of questions asked in the classroom. Teachers must know something about the content to be able to ask these kinds of questions. Such questions tend to be closed-ended; that is, only a finite and well-defined set

of answers will satisfy them. On the other hand, process questions (such as those in Conversation B) tend to be open-ended; the questioner can draw out relevant information, organize and analyze it, and ask questions without knowing the content. The teacher in Conversation B is more effective at encouraging the answerer (in this case, the student) to do his own thinking to arrive at conclusions.

Content questions are a necessary part of our questioning repertoire, whether we're problem solving or not. They are, however, not sufficient; they have limitations. To rely primarily on content questions is equivalent to trying to build a house with only a hammer. We can do a lot of things with that hammer, but we will also leave a lot undone.

Process questions have the following characteristics:

• *Have a purpose.* Contrary to some questioning strategies that emphasize the quantity or type of questions asked, problem-solving questions focus on the purpose of the question. If we know exactly what kind of information or input we are looking for, we are able to modify or develop questions that will help us achieve our goal. To resolve an issue, the result of the questioning, not the activity of questioning, is important; that is, questioning is important because of the information we obtain, the judgments we make, and the way we involve others.

Each of our four analytic processes has an overall purpose or goal, and each step or question within the process clearly contributes to that goal. Good questioning for issue resolution means that every question has a clear-cut purpose and that we question until that purpose is met. Knowing the purpose allows us to better form the question.

• *Are effectively sequenced or organized.* Once the purpose of the questions is clear, we can effectively sequence the questions we ask. Many questioning strategies don't emphasize the need for a sequence or pattern of questions. Research suggests that teacher effectiveness increases when the questions follow some kind of rhythm or pattern and when some purpose exists for asking those questions (Wilen, 1991). When we solve problems, the sequence of the questions is critical. The problem-solving processes themselves provide the rationale for sequencing the questions. For example, in decision analysis, we need to understand the objectives or goals for the decision before we can effectively evaluate the options. Therefore, questions about objectives must precede questions about alternatives. Random questioning increases the chances that we will overlook critical data and waste valuable time and resources.

• *Effectively involve others.* Effective use of questioning in problem solving presumes that we may need information, ideas, and the involvement of others. But we all know people whose actions suggest they don't value involvement. Those people engage in the following practices:

○ They don't ask questions of others; they make decisions themselves.

○ They ask others but disregard or ignore others' input.

○ They ask leading questions that belie their bias and encourage others to concur.

What results from these actions? People who do not involve others lose the opportunity to improve the quality of their solution. They typically receive limited support for their solutions. They pay the price during implementation as they try to force, cajole, or convince others, after the fact, that their choice is correct. People who pretend to value others' input and then ignore it engender resentment and, ultimately, cynicism from those with whom they work. Those who co-opt others through leading questions tend to think they have support when they really don't. By never honestly seeking others' input—only their tacit agreement—these individuals create feelings of disenfranchisement in colleagues and subordinates.

Seeking others' input doesn't mean we have to use it or agree with it—just that we consider it. Questioners must value what the answerer has to offer, whether it is data, opinions, observations, or ideas. In problem solving, if we do not value the answers, the questions become an exercise in irrelevance, and the opportunity for learning (for both questioner and answerer) is lost.

Research has demonstrated that both teachers and students can be encouraged to learn and apply the skill of asking effective questions. One study shows that when this skill was taught, students were able to effectively ask critical questions. The more they practiced the skill (i.e., the more questions they asked), the better their questions were. They were much more engaged in the learning process (Cecil, 1995).

We believe it is vital for all of us to develop the ability to ask effective questions. This ability is particularly important if we are to be effective in resolving the issues that confront us. After all, successful issue resolution requires us to effectively involve others and obtain and analyze relevant information. How else can we accomplish this task than by asking the right questions?

In the next four chapters, we look more closely at the four analytic processes for issue resolution and the questions that make up each of these processes.

Decision Analysis: What's Our Best Choice?

From a very early age, we make decisions daily. These decisions are often routine, inconsequential choices we are barely aware of making (e.g., what to wear, when to leave the house for work or school, or whether to eat lunch). Sometimes they are less clear-cut and may have a significant effect on us or others (e.g., whether or not to go to school or work, how to best raise student achievement, or how to raise money for a class trip). Sometimes decisions that appear fairly simple can be life changing (e.g., deciding to participate in a prank that goes awry, choosing to drive drunk, or determining how to handle a crisis).

The nature of the decision and the criticality of the outcome may differ, but each decision is characterized by certain elements:

• The need to make a choice between two or more possible courses of action.
• Objectives or criteria that define a successful decision or solution.
• Consequences associated with each possible choice.

Decision making is at least in part about making trade-offs. Rarely are we given a perfect option—an alternative that perfectly satisfies or meets all our criteria. Typically, certain options meet some criteria better than others. How do we make decisions about the criteria? How do we decide we would rather give up some of this in order to have some of that?

Decision making involves making wise decisions about our trade-offs. Effective decision

28

making entails being aware of and adequately considering each element of the decision. Our research shows that effective decision makers consider all these elements in arriving at a choice. But they are often unable to articulate what they did to reach that choice. Effective decision makers are characterized by their ability to

- Clearly recognize that a choice needs to be made.
- Thoroughly consider the objectives or criteria that define a successful choice.
- Identify all possible options or alternatives.
- Use criteria to evaluate each alternative.
- Consider the risks associated with a given alternative.
- Clearly articulate their final choice.
- Involve others where and when necessary in the decision-making process.

Pitfalls in Decision Making

We all have made decisions that did not turn out the way we had hoped. Or we have watched others make decisions and wondered what they could possibly have been thinking. Several common pitfalls can reduce the quality of the end result. Here are some of them and the effect they can have on our decisions:

- *Jumping to alternatives.* When we need to make a decision, we typically start by analyzing the alternatives. In a group, someone will often advocate for a favored alternative or option. Others will agree or disagree, pointing out why that is or is not a good choice. The emotional intensity of the discussion increases as participants become more personally invested in the choices they are advocating or opposing. Reaching consensus becomes increasingly difficult as people become polarized.

When we jump to an alternative, we often fail to consider a robust range of options. We become so focused on critiquing a single alternative that we don't think carefully about whether other ways to accomplish the task exist or what other options we have.

Perhaps the biggest drawback of jumping to an alternative is that we have not thoroughly considered what is important in a final choice. We critique or advocate alternatives without agreeing on or being clear about how to evaluate those alternatives.

- *Inadequately specifying the purpose for a decision.* A related pitfall in decision making occurs when we fail to think through what we want and need in a final choice. How would we define the ideal alternative? What would it look like? By not making these qualities and considerations explicit, we inconsistently evaluate each alternative. Such inconsistency is what happens with the common pro-con analysis. When we don't specify our purpose, we focus on the alternatives without adequately considering what we need to achieve or what would be true in an ideal choice. The result is that each alternative, in effect, receives a separate analysis. We do not evaluate alternatives using a common set of criteria. Not having a stated purpose is equivalent to grading papers using a separate rubric for each individual paper. How can we give a grade that everyone will understand if our standards are different for each paper?
- *Ineffectively using information.* In our data-rich world, sorting out the information we need to make a good decision can be difficult. We have access to the information we need, but we are not

clear on what that information is and how to get it. We may get too much information about some points and not enough about other critical points. It is easy to confuse quantity of information with its relevancy and quality. Making a decision without enough of the right information invariably affects the quality of the outcome.

• *Not considering the consequences of a decision.* In our quest to arrive at a decision, we frequently overlook the potential risks inherent within our choice, until we are actually living with the consequences. These are the decisions that, once implemented, cause those cries of dismay: How could I have done that? How could they possibly have decided this? What could they have been thinking?

• *Not recognizing that we have options.* Sometimes we do not realize we have choices in a given situation. We do things the way they have always been done or because we believe that is what is expected. When we fail to recognize that choices are available, we might miss the opportunity for new or creative ways to address an issue.

• *Failing to effectively involve others.* We often fail to recognize the necessity and value of involving others in the decision-making process. The results can be decisions that are not well thought out or that are not supported by others. Effective involvement of others in the process can not only improve the quality of the solution, but also increase the chances that a decision will be supported and implemented.

A Scenario for Decision Analysis

Joe is a college-bound high school senior who needs to make a decision soon about which school he wants to attend. He has been rejected by his first-choice school, but several other colleges and universities have accepted him. To hold his place at one of these schools, he needs to send a deposit shortly. He and his parents discuss the situation over dinner:

Joe: I'm having trouble making up my mind about where I want to go to school. This is a huge decision. I know I really like Pleasant U. And people have said good things about Castle College, too.

Paul (Joe's dad): Why not Mercy U.? You got in there, too, and it's a much better school.

Linda (Joe's mom): Paul, that's so far away. I hate the idea of my baby being so far from home.

Paul: Honestly, Linda, the boy is 18 years old. He needs to get out on his own. When I was his age, you were considered a man at 18. As you know, I was married and supporting a family at 19.

Linda: Times have changed, though. Joe, what do you think about Haven U.? Susie goes there and really likes it.

Joe: Susie just likes it because she's on the swim team. Besides, it's too small.

Linda: It does have a nationally ranked swim team, Joe.

Joe: Mom, I don't even swim.

Paul: Mercy is 300 miles away; that's close enough to visit but far enough to feel like you're somewhere new. It's a good school. I hear they have an incredible library, too. I am really concerned about your interest in Pleasant U.

Joe: What's wrong with Pleasant U.? You automatically just write it off because you want me to go to Mercy.

Paul: I'm not writing it off. I just don't think you're being rational. Pleasant is a fine school, but not for someone of your caliber.

Joe: You don't even know what's important to me. All you care about is your own opinion. Forget trying to talk about this. I'll just make my decision on my own.

Paul: Not if you're expecting us to contribute anything toward your education. If we're helping pay for tuition, we all need to be involved.

Joe: Fine, you decide then. *Joe gets up and leaves the table.*

Does this exchange sound familiar? The content may be different from other decision-making situations you have encountered, but undoubtedly, some of the pitfalls and difficulties are the same. Let's look at what we can observe about this exchange:

- True to fashion, the first things discussed are the alternatives. Everyone jumps right in to propose an alternative (in this case, a college) and suggest a reason it might be the best choice.
- The emotional level rises as Joe and his parents begin to lobby for their favored alternative and denigrate others. When they feel misunderstood, they tend to defend themselves rather than listen to other opinions.
- There does not appear to be common understanding or agreement as to what each would like to have in a college. The situation

begs the questions, What does Joe want in a college? What is important to him? What do his parents think he needs to consider?

The Steps in Decision Analysis

Decision analysis is a process that uses questions to help avoid the typical pitfalls of decision making and maximize the chances for success. By incorporating the components of effective decision making, it allows all stakeholders to become better decision makers.

Decision making selects the best option or alternative. We use the acronym SELECT to help remind us of the basic purpose of this process. Each letter in the acronym stands for a key decision-making step (shown earlier in Figure 1.4):

- **S**tate the decision.
- **E**stablish and classify objectives.
- **L**ist alternatives.
- **E**valuate alternatives.
- **C**onsider risks.
- **T**rust your work—pick a winner!

In this section, we look at each step in the decision analysis process and show how it might apply in an actual decision-making situation. We discuss the key questions each step is designed to answer and the purpose or rationale that underlies each step. We look at how this process applies to a situation already introduced—Joe's college choice dilemma.

State the Decision

This step answers the key question, What are we trying to decide? or What statement best describes the choice we need to make? Clearly identifying the choice we face is important. Not only do we acknowledge that we need to make a choice, but we also keep focused on the decision at hand. A simple statement can usually capture the overall intent or purpose for our decision; however, clarifying this purpose is not always easy.

The way we state the decision also affects the range of alternatives we consider. For example, if Joe's decision were stated as, Decide whether or not to go to Pleasant U., the phrasing would indicate that he was considering only two alternatives—going to Pleasant U. or not going. Such phrasing limits our choices and discourages creative thinking about alternatives. If we reworded his statement to, Decide what to do after graduating from high school, we would expand the options to include going to junior college, working and then going to college, working full time, going to a trade school, and so forth. In this particular situation, though, Joe seems to be trying to decide which four-year college or university to attend.

Applying the Process:
College Decision Example

We might state the decision Joe faces as, Choose a four-year college or university to attend. However we word the statement, we want to accurately reflect the overall intent or purpose of the decision (i.e., choosing a college) and make sure we consider an appropriate range of alternatives. For example, if Joe is unwilling to consider any option that is not a four-year college, why state the decision as, Choose what to do after high school? We would be considering several options that are not viable for Joe at this time.

Establish and Classify Objectives

We *establish* objectives or criteria by asking the key question, What do we want or need in a final choice? The objectives we identify become the foundation for evaluating alternatives. Sometimes the objectives help create or suggest other alternatives.

When we *classify* objectives, we ask, Which objectives are mandatory? How will we measure them? Objectives that are mandatory *and* measurable in a clear-cut way are *musts*. All other objectives are *wants*. When we classify our objectives, we identify the minimum requirements any alternative must meet. Thus, we do not consider any options that do not meet certain minimum standards. On the other hand, although we may be tempted to classify all important objectives as *musts*, we need to remember that this approach may unnecessarily restrict the alternatives we evaluate.

The more completely we establish and classify our objectives, the better our chance to select the best possible alternative. This is the time to dream. What would our ideal alternative look like and accomplish? We may not be able to find a perfect alternative, but why not get as close as possible?

Applying the Process:
College Decision Example

To establish an initial list of objectives, Joe asks himself variations of the key questions: What do I want in a college? What is important for me to consider in choosing a college? What do others say I should keep in mind? Then he lists his objectives:

- More than 5,000 students.
- Good academic reputation.
- Beautiful setting.

- Good athletic facilities.
- Acceptable distance from home.

Joe shows this list to his parents, and they suggest some additional objectives that he agrees are important. His final list looks like this:

- More than 5,000 students.
- Good academic reputation.
- Beautiful setting.
- Good athletic facilities.
- Friendly atmosphere.
- Acceptable distance from home.
- Good selection of extracurricular activities.
- Total tuition cost to us of less than $12,000 per year (with or without financial aid).
- Strong alumni network.
- Desirable student housing.
- Minimal cost.

Joe and his parents classify his objectives. The *musts* (M) they initially identify are these:

- (M) More than 5,000 students.
- (M) Total tuition cost to us of less than $12,000 per year (with or without financial aid).

Joe is adamant that the college be an acceptable distance from home. These questions must be answered: What is acceptable? How will he recognize it when he sees it? To give distance a measurable limit, he decides that a college needs to be at least a two-hour drive from home, but no more than six hours. Those distances provide a clear-cut measure that he can easily use to determine whether a school meets this *must*. Were he not able to identify a clear-cut measure for a *must*, the objective would be a *want*.

At first glance, the objectives "total tuition cost to us of less than $12,000 per year" and "minimal cost" may seem redundant. But because one is a *must* and one is a *want*, they serve different functions. The *must* objective indicates that Joe and his family are willing to spend no more than

$12,000 each year on tuition. All acceptable alternatives must have tuition costs of less than $12,000; the *want* objective indicates it would be nice to conserve money if possible. Therefore, the less expensive the tuition costs, the better an alternative would satisfy the tuition cost objective. For example, a college that costs $7,000 each year will satisfy the *want* objective better than a college that costs $11,000 each year.

Joe's classified list of objectives looks like this:

- (M) More than 5,000 students.
- (M) Two to six hours from home.
- (M) Total tuition cost to us of less than $12,000 per year (with and without financial aid).
- Good academic reputation.
- Beautiful setting.
- Good athletic facilities.
- Friendly atmosphere.
- Good selection of extracurricular activities.
- Strong alumni network.
- Desirable student housing.
- Minimal cost.

List Alternatives

This step answers the key question, What alternatives should we consider? We list alternatives so that we are clear about what choices are available. Sometimes we are given the alternatives from which to choose. At other times, we may need to search out alternatives or even create them for ourselves. Typically, identifying alternatives is not difficult.

Applying the Process:
College Decision Example

In Joe's case, deciding on alternatives is an easy step. He knows that he wants to go to one of the four colleges to which he was accepted; he's just not sure which one. The schools that accepted him are Pleasant U., Mercy U., Haven U., and Castle College.

Evaluate Alternatives

Evaluating alternatives helps us assess how well our identified alternatives meet our objectives or criteria. First, we record information about how each alternative meets our *musts*, and we ask the key question, Does this alternative satisfy this *must* objective? If the answer is yes, we continue to consider the alternative. If the answer is no, we drop the alternative from further consideration. Remember, the *musts* represent what we must have in our final choice. If an alternative doesn't meet these requirements, it is not viable. We do not waste time by examining it further.

For the remaining alternatives, we ask, How well does each alternative meet each *want*? We then gather and record relevant information. If we focus on the information that relates to our objectives, we ensure that the information we get is directly relevant to our decision.

We suggest using a matrix, such as the one shown in Figure 3.1 (pp. 36–37), to organize and analyze the information. The matrix lays out the relevant information, shows specifically what information we may be missing, and allows us to see how well our alternatives meet our objectives.

Applying the Process:
College Decision Example

Joe reviews his notes, recollections, and reference materials to obtain information he needs to complete this step: Evaluate alternatives. The matrix in Figure 3.1 clarifies exactly what information he has and what, specifically, he is missing. When the information is not readily accessible, Joe is able to easily form a question or conduct a search that helps him obtain the missing pieces of information. He quickly eliminates one of his choices (Haven U.) because it does not meet his *must* of having more than 5,000 students.

Once Joe has obtained and organized the information he has about each remaining alternative and how it meets each objective, he can take a more rational look at his choices. He is struck by how well Castle College seems to meet his objectives. Joe hadn't looked too closely at Castle. He had spent a lot of energy pushing for Pleasant U. He had a good experience when he went to visit, and he kept looking for other reasons to support his leanings. Conversely, he was looking for reasons to discount Mercy U., where he felt his dad was pressuring him to go. Sometimes in the struggle to defend one alternative or disregard another, we may overlook an excellent possibility.

Consider Risks

For each alternative we are still considering we ask the key question, What could go wrong if we choose this alternative? Have you ever watched people charge ahead with what seemed like great solutions, only to discover huge problems they hadn't considered? These big problems often arise during implementation, and we wonder, How could they not have seen this coming? When we identify the risks associated with an alternative, we can balance our decision making. Sometimes a risk is so great we are prompted to choose a different alternative. At other times, we may decide that the risks associated with an alternative are not prohibitive, and because we identified them in advance, we can minimize the chances that problems will occur.

Applying the Process:
College Decision Example

Joe reflects on his experiences and research and identifies some risks associated with the three remaining alternatives:

• *Pleasant University.* When Joe checks around more, he finds that Pleasant U.'s academic status is about to be downgraded by a nationally recognized source.

• *Mercy University.* A lot of animosity exists between the college and the town. Apparently, tensions have been escalating and the situation has become increasingly uncomfortable for Mercy students. In addition, construction is scheduled to begin on a major new library addition. Experts predict that it will take three years to complete the project.

• *Castle College.* The tuition cost is close to Joe's $12,000 limit. If for some reason he does not get sufficient aid in subsequent years, or if the college raises tuition sufficiently, this limit might be exceeded.

Trust Your Work—Pick a Winner!

The key questions we ask are these: Which alternative should we choose? Which alternative provides the best balance of benefits and risks? Ultimately, we need to commit to a choice or alternative. Therefore, we need to take the analysis that we have done and determine which alternative will work best for us.

Applying the Process:
College Decision Example

Joe reviews his options, the way they perform against his objectives, and the risks they each carry. The primary risk associated with Castle involves a possible tuition increase. Joe checks around and finds that tuition has increased for the past three years at an average of $200 each year. With the last increase, the college vowed not to increase tuition for two years. The financial aid office informs Joe that as long as a student maintains the acceptable grade-point average, the only reason the college might cut back on aid would be for disciplinary problems. Lastly, Joe consults his parents, who inform him that $12,000 per year is the maximum they can afford at this time. They are willing to prepare for a possible future increase by putting aside some additional funds in subsequent years. Given how well Castle meets his objectives, and given that the risks seem manageable, Joe and his parents decide that Castle is the best college for him.

Decision Analysis Refinements

Sometimes, decisions are so complex or critical that we need some additional tools to help us manage and make sense of information. Figure 3.2 (p. 38) shows where refinements fit within the flow of decision analysis steps.

Weighing the *Wants*

Typically, the *want* objectives we have identified are not equally important. Weighing the *wants* is a technique that allows us to reflect on their relative importance.

FIGURE 3.1
Evaluating Alternatives in the College Decision Example

Objective	Must Objectives (M)	Alternative 1: Pleasant U. Must Objective Met?	Alternative 1: Pleasant U. Description/Evaluation	Alternative 2: Mercy U. Must Objective Met?	Alternative 2: Mercy U. Description/Evaluation	Alternative 3: Haven U. Must Objective Met?	Alternative 3: Haven U. Description/Evaluation	Alternative 4: Castle College Must Objective Met?	Alternative 4: Castle College Description/Evaluation
More than 5,000 students	M	Yes.	7,500 students.	Yes.	15,000 students.	No.	3,500 students.	Yes.	5,500 students.
Two to six hours from home	M	Yes.	Three-hour drive.	Yes.	Six-hour drive.			Yes.	Four-hour drive.
Total tuition cost to us of less than $12,000/year	M	Yes.	$5,000 (in-state students; no aid available).	Yes.	$9,500 (thanks to financial aid package).			Yes.	$11,500 (thanks to financial aid package).
Good academic reputation			Fair.		Excellent.				Excellent.
Beautiful setting			Beautiful countryside; rolling hills.		Attractive.				Very pretty; small town.
Good athletic facilities			Excellent; new field house.		Good; wide range of facilities.				Very good; new gym will be completed in two years.

FIGURE 3.1
(continued)

Objective	Must Objectives (M)	Alternative 1: Pleasant U. Must Objective Met?	Alternative 1: Pleasant U. Description/ Evaluation	Alternative 2: Mercy U. Must Objective Met?	Alternative 2: Mercy U. Description/ Evaluation	Alternative 3: Haven U. Must Objective Met?	Alternative 3: Haven U. Description/ Evaluation	Alternative 4: Castle College Must Objective Met?	Alternative 4: Castle College Description/ Evaluation
Friendly atmosphere			Students very friendly.		Fairly friendly; feels more anonymous because of size.				Very friendly; everyone seems to love it.
Good selection of extra-curricular activities			Pretty good, especially in sports; other offerings a little sparse.		Excellent; many clubs and intramural sports.				Excellent; outing club very strong.
Strong alumni network			Fairly weak; alumni seem uninvolved.		Strong; lots of activities.				For a small school, seems especially strong.
Desirable student housing			New dorms; variety of possibilities.		Wide range of theme housing; lots of fraternities.				Good ones off campus; limited on-campus housing.
Minimal cost			Tuition: $5,000.		Tuition: $9,500.				Tuition: $11,500.

Note: Haven U. does not meet the *must* objective, so Joe eliminated it from further consideration.

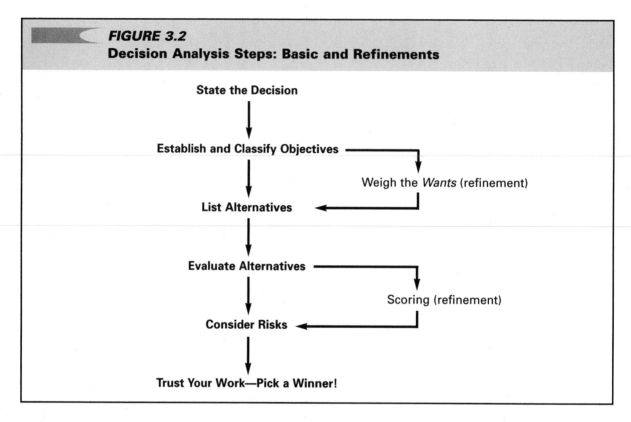

FIGURE 3.2
Decision Analysis Steps: Basic and Refinements

State the Decision

Establish and Classify Objectives

Weigh the *Wants* (refinement)

List Alternatives

Evaluate Alternatives

Scoring (refinement)

Consider Risks

Trust Your Work—Pick a Winner!

We ask the key question, Which *wants* (or *want*) are most important? Then we ask, Compared to our most important *wants*, how important is each other *want?* We assign each *want* a weight between 10 (most important) and 1 (slightly important).

Applying the Process: College Decision Example

Joe weighs his *want* objectives and then shows them to his parents for their reaction. They test his thinking against a couple of the weights he has identified; his final list looks like this:

- (M) More than 5,000 students.
- (M) Two to six hours from home.
- (M) Tuition cost to us of less than $12,000 per year.
- (10) Good academic reputation.
- (4) Beautiful setting.
- (6) Good athletic facilities.
- (10) Friendly atmosphere.
- (8) Good selection of extracurricular activities.
- (2) Strong alumni network.
- (6) Desirable student housing.
- (5) Minimal cost.

Scoring the Alternatives

If we have weighed our *want* objectives (see previous step), we use scoring to evaluate the alternatives to get a clearer picture of how well our alternatives perform.

First, we screen our alternatives against our *musts* and record relevant information. (See *musts* columns in Figure 3.1.) Again, Haven U. does not meet the *must* objective of "more than 5,000 students," so it is eliminated from further consideration. Then, we consider each *want* and ask the key question, Which alternative best meets this *want* objective? We score that alternative as a 10.

We ask the question, Compared to our best-performing alternatives, how well do our other alternatives perform? Give each alternative a score between 10 (equally well) and 0 (not at all).

We calculate the weighted score by multiplying the weight of the objective by the score of the alternative. We calculate the total weighted score for each alternative by adding its weighted scores.

Applying the Process: College Decision Example

If Joe used the refinement, scoring the alternatives, Figure 3.3 (pp. 40–41) shows what his evaluation of the alternatives might look like.

As Joe tabulates the scores, he is surprised and pleased to see how well Castle College performs against his objectives. It is the top-performing alternative for both of his most important objectives. After scoring the alternatives, Joe considers the risks (see Consider Risks section discussed earlier in the chapter) before making his final choice.

Involving Others in Decision Making

Many decisions fail because the right people were not adequately involved. Some decisions we can and must make on our own. But under certain conditions, we should involve others in the decision-making process. Here are some of these conditions:

• Others have information, expertise, or experience we need to effectively establish objectives, identify and evaluate alternatives, and assess risks.
• We need someone else's buy-off or approval to move forward.
• We need help or commitment from others to effectively implement the decision.
• A high-quality resolution is needed (the decision may be highly visible, complicated, and significant).

When one or more of these conditions exist, we must involve others in our decision making. Such efforts do not necessarily mean gathering all 200 stakeholders in one room and proceeding through a full-blown analysis. We can involve others one-on-one, in small groups, or in larger groups by the following means:

• Asking for information and expertise.
• Asking for feedback and opinions on work conducted so far.
• Asking for approval or buy-off.
• Asking for help in gathering or analyzing information.

We can also involve others at each step in the decision analysis process. For example, when we establish and classify objectives, we want to include the objectives of those who may be affected by the decision. We need to ask ourselves, Who has experience or information we might need? Whose commitment do we need for approval and implementation of whatever we

FIGURE 3.3
Scoring Alternatives in the College Decision Example

Want Objective	Weight of Objective[1]	Alternative 1: Pleasant U.			Alternative 2: Mercy U.			Alternative 3: Castle College		
		Description/ Evaluation	Score of Alternative[2]	Weighted Score	Description/ Evaluation	Score of Alternative[2]	Weighted Score	Description/ Evaluation	Score of Alternative[2]	Weighted Score
Good academic reputation	10	Fair.	5	50	Excellent.	10	100	Excellent.	10	100
Beautiful setting	4	Beautiful countryside; rolling hills.	10	40	Attractive.	1	4	Very pretty; small town	8	32
Good athletic facilities	6	Excellent; new field house.	10	60	Good; wide range of facilities.	6	36	Very good; new gym will be completed in two years.	8	48
Friendly atmosphere	10	Students very friendly.	10	100	Fairly friendly; feels more anonymous because of size.	7	70	Very friendly; everyone seems to love it.	10	100
Good selection of extracurricular activities	8	Pretty good, especially in sports; other offerings a little sparse.	6	48	Excellent; many clubs and intramural sports.	10	80	Excellent; outing club very strong.	10	80

FIGURE 3.3
(continued)

Want Objective	Weight of Objective[1]	Alternative 1: Pleasant U.			Alternative 2: Mercy U.			Alternative 3: Castle College		
		Description/ Evaluation	Score of Alternative[2]	Weighted Score	Description/ Evaluation	Score of Alternative[2]	Weighted Score	Description/ Evaluation	Score of Alternative[2]	Weighted Score
Strong alumni network	2	Fairly weak; alumni seem uninvolved.	2	4	Strong; lots of activities.	10	20	For a small school, seems especially strong.	8	16
Desirable student housing	6	New dorms; variety of possibilities.	8	48	Wide range of theme housing; lots of fraternities.	10	60	Good ones off campus; limited on-campus housing.	6	36
Minimal cost	5	Tuition: $5,000.	10	50	Tuition: $9,500.	7	35	Tuition: $11,500.	5	25
		Total Weighted Score		400	Total Weighted Score		405	Total Weighted Score		437

[1]Objectives are weighed using a scale of 10 (most important) to 1 (slightly important).
[2]Alternatives are scored using a scale of 10 (best alternative to meet this objective) to 0 (alternative does not meet this objective at all).

choose? Who needs to be included to demonstrate objectivity of the process? Who is seen as a leader and a person with influence (e.g., who is important to involve)? Whose approval of the objectives do we need before we move forward?

When we effectively involve others, we improve the *quality* of our end result. In addition, we can increase others' *commitment* to a final choice. These two factors can mean the difference between a decision that looks good on paper and one that actually gets implemented successfully. We sometimes use lack of time as a reason not to involve others. Yet we seem to have time to try to sell the decision to others or force them to implement it. Even though involving others may take more time up front, it will save time during implementation because it ensures a high-quality solution that others understand and are willing to support.

Applying Decision Analysis in Schools

As with many methodologies, decision analysis makes conceptual sense. Conceptual integrity, however, is seldom reason enough to take a leap into the unknown. Rather, we're more likely to try new things if we believe they will result in actual or potential benefits for others or ourselves. We discussed previously what administrators, teachers, and others have reported about the benefits of using the four analytic tools. We next look at situations in which administrators and teachers found decision analysis a useful tool or skill. First, we examine examples of how decision analysis ideas have been used by administrators in school or district settings. Then we look at examples of how decision analysis has been used with and by students.

Examples of Administrative Use

Making scheduling decisions. A California high school set up a task force to investigate restructuring as a means to school improvement. The task force explored many facets of restructuring but decided its top priority was to look at extended class time.

Using research and input from others, the task force agreed on a decision statement and objectives. These were shared with the faculty, and their input was solicited. Here is the final decision statement: Decide which framework of instructional time best supports the restructuring initiative of the high school and also meets the required number of instructional minutes according to the California education code. The task force wanted to provide a schedule that met these objectives:

- Allows time for teachers to confer with individual students.
- Allows time for students to carry out independent research and participate in school-to-career experiences.
- Allows teachers to plan collaboratively in developing thematic units.
- Allows teachers to team-teach thematic units.
- Allows time throughout the school day for staff to participate in professional growth opportunities.
- Allows extended class time to meet instructional and content needs.
- Allows students to concentrate on fewer classes at one time.
- Maximizes instruction with a lower student-to-teacher ratio.
- Allows for a comprehensive senior project or demonstration for the graduation portfolio.

The task force learned through its discussions with faculty that some departments were more opposed to a scheduling change than others. Consequently, the task force created a way to receive departmental input and see where the differences lay by having each department weigh the objectives using a scale of 10 (most important) to 1 (slightly important). Then the averages for each objective were calculated to get a sense of relative priority of the objectives. The results are shown in Figure 3.4 (p. 44).

The task force presented three alternative scheduling systems for consideration. Over the next few months, teams researched the different alternatives and made site visits to schools that used the various systems. The task force's research added new alternatives for participants to consider (primarily variations on the three major systems). Here are the alternatives they ultimately evaluated:

- Their current system (traditional six periods).
- Block (two-day).
- Block (four-day).
- Block (five-day).
- Two-day block with intersession (an intersession is a miniblock of time used for remediation or an elective).
- Four-day block with intersession.
- Five-day block with intersession.
- Current schedule with intersession.
- Copernican (three classes per quarter with an intersession).

Task force members decided to use a variation for their evaluation. Rather than have every person evaluate each alternative, they devised a modified means to determine each person's feeling about each alternative. After the task force presented the results to the faculty, each person was asked to provide a general rating for each alternative on a scale of 1 (unacceptable) to 5 (highly acceptable). Participants were encouraged to use the objectives identified earlier to make their assessments. In an unprecedented level of acceptance for such a controversial change, the faculty endorsed the Copernican plan, with an 81 percent rating of highly acceptable.

The task would have been much faster and simpler had the administrators just decided to move the high school to a block-scheduling plan. But the time and effort saved up front would surely have been expended during implementation, getting people to accept and like an option they were vigorously opposed to. When we make significant decisions that require support of others, it is almost always easier to get people involved and committed than to clean up the ill will that a poorly conceived decision can create.

Making hiring decisions. At Whitman Middle School (Wauwatosa, Wisconsin), a hiring team used decision analysis to select a new building library aide. The team established, classified, and weighed the objectives. They determined that they wanted an individual with the following characteristics and skills:

- (M) Proper license and qualifications.
- (10) People skills.
- (10) Flexibility.
- (9) Experience in schools.
- (9) Knowledge of this age group (i.e., middle school students).
- (8) Organizational skills.
- (7) Desire to learn.
- (7) Computer skills.

FIGURE 3.4
Weighing Objectives in the Scheduling Decision Example

Objectives for a Schedule	DEPARTMENT AND WEIGHT OF OBJECTIVE*						
	English	Foreign Language	History/ Social Science	Math	Science	Other	Average
Allows time for teachers to confer with individual students.	10	3	2	9	10	6	6.66
Allows time for students to carry out independent research and participate in school-to-career experiences.	5	4	8	2	7	5	5.16
Allows teachers to plan collaboratively in developing thematic units.	7	9	2	2	8	6	5.66
Allows teachers to team-teach thematic units.	7	6	4	1	8	6	5.33
Allows time throughout the school day for staff to participate in professional growth opportunities.	3	2	1	8	6	6	4.33
Allows extended class time to meet instructional and content needs.	8	10	5	6	10	9	8.00
Allows students to concentrate on fewer classes at one time.	8	9	10	1	8	8	7.33
Maximizes instruction with a lower student-to-teacher ratio.	10	7	10	10	8	10	9.16
Allows time for a comprehensive senior project or demonstration for the graduation portfolio.	5	5	6	1	7	5	4.83

*Scale for weighing objectives: 10 = most important; 1 = slightly important.

- (6) Word processing skills.
- (5) Physically capable.
- (5) Knowledge of library.
- (4) Internet skills.

The team then developed questions to use in interviewing candidates. Members used the objectives to develop the questions. Because the team knew what it was looking for in a library aide (i.e., the objectives), the questions ensured that they would get relevant information (i.e., information that corresponds to their objectives). Here are sample interview questions:

- What is something new you have learned recently, and how did it apply to your job?
- What does the word *flexibility* mean to you? Please describe two situations where you had to be flexible.
- What are typical characteristics of a middle school child?
- Based on the characteristics you have described above, how do you structure children's time in the library?
- What characteristics do you want the people you work with to possess?
- What is some background information that you'd like to share that highlights your experiences related to middle school?

The team interviewed the candidates and evaluated and scored them using a matrix. They considered risks for their top-performing candidates and made a final selection. They reported the following benefits:

- Decision analysis helped keep the decision from being a purely emotional one.

- Objectives established before hiring helped better structure the hiring process and make it more objective.
- The process provided a common language and approach.
- The process provided an equal say in the decision from all parties involved.
- They have confidence the best person was hired.
- The process helped explain and clarify for others why this person was chosen and other people were not.

Designing or creating new alternatives. In Brighton, Michigan, a planning team was charged with designing a new alternative: determining the best approach to qualify a student as learning disabled. The approach they had used previously did not meet the needs of various stakeholders. The team developed a list of objectives. Their *must* objectives included the following:

- Meets state guidelines.
- Meets federal guidelines.
- Meets Livingston Educational Service Agency (LESA) guidelines.

Their *want* objectives included the following:

- Ensures accurate identification of students' disabilities.
- Maximizes communication network with and by the Multidisciplinary Evaluation Team (MET) (the team who determines special education eligibility).
- Focuses on needs of student and what is best.
- Maximizes parental acceptance of diagnosis.

- Maximizes LESA support.
- Maximizes building administration support.
- Maximizes staff support.
- Maximizes staff acceptance of goals.
- Affects the most students (applies to general school population).

Sometimes we need to create our own alternatives. This is true particularly when we develop a new process or approach. In the case above, the list of objectives served as a guide to help create or design a new alternative. To design their own alternative (i.e., a new method for qualifying a student as learning disabled), the Brighton team asked, How can we best meet each objective? What alternative can we put together that will allow us to achieve these objectives? The team made a flowchart that showed both the steps to qualify a student and the person involved at each step. The objectives, in a sense, became the design specifications for the final alternative.

Assessing the recommendations of others. In rapidly growing school systems, school construction can be a highly charged issue. Millions of dollars can be spent to design and build an elementary school that will house fewer than 1,000 students. High schools that serve up to 3,000 students can cost $50 million. Because of the high stakes involved, the process used to select contractors is often contentious and closely scrutinized.

One Florida school district, in keeping with state law, had a procedure to deal with contractor selections. If a selection was challenged, however, district leadership was in an awkward position because they were unable to provide supporting data for their decision. The superin-

tendent asked that a process be created that would make it clear to everyone why certain selections were made. When asked what he was looking for in a process, he said he wanted to be able to answer the following questions:

- What objectives did you consider, and what was the priority for each objective?
- Whose input and involvement did you get in reaching this decision?
- What options or alternatives did you consider?
- What were the risks associated with the possible options?

This district subsequently set up a selection process structured around decision analysis. Now, the school board and superintendent regularly ask these types of questions when they assess others' recommendations for contractors. The result is a clearly defined process that makes thinking visible through concise documentation. The superintendent and school board receive a report that includes the criteria used to make a recommendation, how well each firm performed on each criterion, and the consensus comments of the selection committee members on each firm's qualifications relative to each criterion. The superintendent's and board members' confidence in the process is high because they are able to see the committee's thinking. Complaints from participating firms have dropped to zero; they, too, can see the committee's thinking and know how decisions were made.

Decision analysis can help us better assess the thinking process that others have used. It clearly points out the gaps in the process and the places where some of the information may be soft or erroneous.

Examples of Classroom Use

Teachers may use decision analysis to help students gain a deeper understanding of curriculum material. Students must often examine decisions that others have made or need to make. When students apply decision analysis to actual or hypothetical decisions, they are forced to consider factors that decision makers considered in a given scenario. When students have to work with content within the context of the decision analysis process, they experience and consider the content in new ways. Educators may also use decision analysis to help students make their own decisions (e.g., selecting a topic for a science project or selecting a class officer). We include here examples of how decision analysis has been used with students.

Exploring a hypothetical decision to better appreciate the complexities of a topic. In a foreign language class at the middle school in Montgomery Township, New Jersey, the teacher is trying to encourage students to see language as something more than conjugating unfamiliar verbs and tenses. He wants to build empathy for people of other lands and cultures and begin exploring the psychosocial aspects of language. He organizes the students in groups and sets up a hypothetical situation that uses the following prompt:

In its continuing quest for world peace, the United Nations is studying the possibility of adopting an official language for use among the citizens of the world. You are a member of the prestigious international committee commissioned by the United Nations to determine which language, if any, should be adopted as the official common language for all.

Sample student objectives for a universal language include these:

• It should be one that most people already know or that is as common to as many existing languages as possible.
• It should be a relatively simple one to learn and teach.
• It should avoid dividing a society into those who know it and those who don't.
• It should avoid loss of diversity and personal freedom.
• It should accommodate a variety of people, such as those with disabilities and older people.
• It should have qualified teachers to teach it.
• It should be adaptable to change.
• It should be cost-effective.
• It should avoid problems with compliance.
• It should not damage the old languages or its people.

Some alternatives the students evaluated included sign language, Latin, English, Spanish, and a new artificial language. After comparing the alternatives to the objectives, each group came to a conclusion about what the ideal language choice would be. Students identified risks for their top choices:

• *Sign language.* Its use might cause loss of emotion; power and effect of music and other audible communication modes would be lost.
• *English.* It might be perceived as a political move by a powerful country and would lead to anger, resentment, and possible conflict.

Groups reached different final conclusions. In some cases, group members believed the risks outweighed the benefits of adopting a particular alternative. In other cases, they developed a new alternative. Final choices included these:

• People should keep their own language and adopt either Latin or sign language as a common second language for communication. No loss of personal culture would occur, and politically powerful groups could not benefit at the expense of others.
• People should keep their own language and adopt sign language as the common second language for citizens worldwide.
• People should keep their own language and adopt a Romance combination language (e.g., Esperanto) as a common second language.

The teacher reported the following results:

• Students thoughtfully considered factors that went into each decision (behavior that the teacher found uplifting).
• Most students exhibited a good to great degree of empathy as they tried to put themselves in other people's shoes.
• Students concluded that language and culture are inextricably intertwined.
• Students believed that language use is difficult to legislate.
• Students of all ability levels were involved in the discussion.
• Several students recognized potential consequences of a universal language (e.g., loss of personal history and ethnic diversity).
• Students debated the concept of what makes one language living and one language dead.
• Students gained an understanding of the change inherent in any spoken language over time.

• Students found that this issue was complex, challenging, and emotional.
• Students felt that decision analysis could be used in many practical day-to-day situations.

Understanding stakeholder viewpoints. At John Witherspoon Middle School (Princeton, New Jersey), a civics class took a closer look at the famed *Brown v. Board of Education* Supreme Court decision. The decision challenged the notion of separate but equal facilities that kept whites and blacks segregated in schools and elsewhere. Before they discussed the ruling, the students formed into groups of three to four. Each group represented a different stakeholder viewpoint. Group members developed and weighed objectives from the viewpoint of their stakeholder group. The groups represented African Americans, the Topeka School Board, school-age children, and white Southerners.

In a subsequent class period, the groups were asked to consider which of four options their stakeholder group would choose: keep segregation, keep segregation but make it more equal, integrate immediately, or integrate gradually. Students discussed whether the weights for their group objectives would be different if they were an African American judge who had experienced discrimination. Each group presented its decision to the class, which discussed the risks associated with each option. The teacher then explained the actual Supreme Court decision.

By representing different stakeholder groups, students gained a better understanding of what the concerns of a given group were. As they watched the different presentations, they clearly saw the differences among stakeholder groups. That knowledge helped them gain greater appreciation not only for the political

FIGURE 3.5
1st Graders Evaluate Potential Pets for Franklin the Turtle

Objective	ALTERNATIVES			
	Snake	Tiger	Fish	Puppy
Easy to take care of	Feed once a week.	Needs cage and a lot of food.	Feed each day— clean tank.	Feed and walk twice a day.
Can learn tricks	No.	Yes, like at circus.	No.	Yes.
Fit in apartment	Yes.	Pretty crowded.	Yes.	Yes.
Cute	Slimy.	Baby tigers are cute.	Maybe certain ones are.	Yes.
Not dangerous	Can bite. Can scare someone.	Looks scary. Might go wild.	Not dangerous.	Not dangerous.

Source: Richetti & Sheerin, 1999, p. 61.

climate at the time of the decision, but also for the way the final decision affected different stakeholders.

Even 1st graders make decisions. At Pyles Elementary School (Anaheim, California), a 1st grade class is reading *Franklin Wants a Pet* (Bourgeois, 1999). Franklin the turtle needs to decide what kind of pet he should get. The teacher asks the class a question to elicit some objectives: "What are some things that you would like in a pet?" She writes their responses in a matrix, a graphic organizer that helps validate student responses. She then asks for three or four ideas of pets to consider. Using student input, she fills in the matrix with information about how well each pet meets a given objective. Finally, the class considers risks when she asks, "What could go wrong if Franklin gets a snake?" "How about if he gets a tiger?" The re-

sults of their analysis are shown in Figure 3.5. This technique helps the teacher assess her students' current knowledge about pets, helps the students think through what they should consider when they select one, and gives them a process to use in other decision situations.

Helping students make classroom decisions. Students at Gonzales Middle School (Gonzales, Louisiana) use decision analysis principles to select topics for their science project. They conduct library research and identify three or four possible topics. In groups, they list important objectives to consider in doing a science project, identify *musts* and *wants,* and weigh the *wants.* The students' *musts* include the following concerns:

• Safety.
• Specificity.

- Testability.
- Ability to get needed materials.

Here are the students' *wants* and the weight for each *want:*

- Expenses (5).
- Time factor (1).
- Challenge (6).
- Originality or creativity (10).
- Interest (9).
- Ease in getting materials (3).

Students compare their various topics against the objectives, score each alternative, and select one topic for their science project. The project lends objectivity and structure to what is typically a difficult choice. The teacher states that the students come up with important objectives she hadn't included on her own list.

Understanding the decisions of others. Curricula are filled with examples of decisions others have made. We can apply decision analysis techniques to get a better understanding of a decision a character in a piece of literature makes or an actual decision a former world leader has made. When we understand the factors the decision maker had to consider—the objectives of those involved, the options (or lack thereof), and the associated risks—we better understand the complexities involved and appreciate the dilemma of the decision maker.

For example, a middle school teacher in Philadelphia uses decision analysis to help her students take a closer look at President Harry Truman's decision to drop the atom bomb. Students examine the objectives Truman considered or might have considered (e.g., end the war and minimize loss of innocent lives). They re-

view some of the options Truman considered (e.g., drop the bomb and invade by sea); ask if other options existed that he might have considered but didn't; and review risks Truman was aware of and those he might not have been aware of at the time.

Other student-related examples. Students and teachers can use decision analysis in a variety of situations. Here are examples:

- After taking a skills inventory, students develop objectives for a future career. They research various careers and evaluate how well each potential career meets each objective. They pick their top choice for a career and present to the class information about the career and why they chose it.
- Students in a middle school child care class use decision analysis to determine the best and most appropriate toys to give to preschool children.
- A middle school history teacher uses decision analysis to help students better understand the dilemma faced by the Shakers and the U.S. government when some Shakers were drafted to serve in the Civil War. Although Shakers did not support slavery, their religion forbade them from being affiliated in any way with bloodshed. Lincoln was concerned that by excusing the Shakers from service, the U.S. government would set a dangerous precedent. Students use decision analysis to evaluate objectives and alternatives from both perspectives.
- Middle school science students use decision analysis to evaluate the use of human growth hormone. They consider the objectives of the general population, pharmaceutical companies, and regulatory agencies while they evaluate four different methods to reduce the physical effects of aging.

• In a final exam, high school English students use decision analysis to demonstrate their knowledge of Holden Caulfield in *Catcher in the Rye*. When the novel ends, Holden will be released from the mental hospital in two weeks. As Holden's parents, what would your objectives be? What are Holden's? What should Holden do next? Students work in teams to identify objectives and list and evaluate alternatives. They also consider the risks of various alternatives.

• After reading *Brave New World,* teams of high school language arts students design their own Utopian societies by identifying objectives and designing an alternative Utopia from them.

• A life sciences teacher asks her students to imagine they are responsible for selecting the next animal to be put on the endangered species list. Students develop objectives for their selection. Then they identify possible candidates for endangered species and research them. After they make a final choice, they develop a pamphlet that advertises their choice and communicates pertinent information.

We have seen how decision analysis can help us better think through our goals and what we need to accomplish when we make a decision. We have learned how we can use decision analysis to better understand the goals and considerations of others. History, literature, government, and other areas are filled with the legacy of other people's decisions. If we understand these decisions, we better understand the decision makers, their constraints, and their hopes. When we use decision analysis ourselves, we can make better choices for our future.

Potential Problem Analysis:
What Could Go Wrong?
Guarding Against Future Trouble

An objective without a plan is a dream.

—RODEN, 1987

Dreaming big can be good. Most significant inventions and innovations result from big dreams. Achieving our goals takes more than wishful thinking, though. Planning and preparation pave the way to success. Foresight and preparation ensure that we excel not just at setting goals, but at achieving them as well.

Incomplete or flawed planning can have disastrous results. In *Blunders in International Business*, Ricks (1993) found that people sometimes overlook key factors and steps in even the largest ventures:

• Before a newly constructed timber mill in East Africa sawed its first log, a French company had to shut it down. Company officials were set for the grand opening when they realized that not enough electricity was available to run the plant. The mill was torn down.

• When United Airlines began to fly from Hong Kong, employees distributed white carnations. Managers couldn't determine why they had problems getting people to fly until someone informed them that Asians often associate these flowers with bad luck and death.

Schools are not immune to such problems. For example, a school district decided to address the problem of student tardiness by locking all classrooms after the bells rang. The plan was quickly scrapped after school officials found that not only did truancy increase, so did vandalism and substance abuse. One student who was locked out of class was later arrested for car theft.

What do these scenarios have in common? All are examples of good intentions gone wrong or good ideas compromised during implementation. An idea on paper can seem brilliant, but we often don't see its limitations until we have to make the idea work. Or we may take some action to solve one problem and unintentionally create new ones.

After a problem erupts, understanding why we could not or did not anticipate it is hard. Yet when we make a decision, the future is unknown. Until a situation goes wrong, the inevitability of that happening is not clear. The challenge is, how do we look into the future to more effectively anticipate and plan for what it may hold?

Potential problem analysis is a tool that can help us maximize our chance of future success when we implement a decision, change, or action. Changes can create multiple problems, but these problems are often preventable. Potential problem analysis helps us avoid future problems and minimize their effects if they do occur.

Looking Back on a Situation Gone Wrong

We sometimes don't understand how the decision makers could have overlooked elements that seem obvious. But when we look at the dynamics of decision making and implementation, this lack is easier to understand. Here are some reasons we don't do a better job of planning for successful implementation:

- *We are exhausted when we arrive at a decision.* Making a difficult or controversial decision is often taxing. If we have done a good job, we have involved key stakeholders, anticipated and addressed objections, used data, made revisions, and obtained necessary approvals. For major decisions, this process typically takes time and is subject to intense scrutiny. By the time we have agreed on an option, we are tempted to just breathe a sigh of relief and move on. Continuing to examine a situation we view as resolved can be difficult. In reality, once the decision is made, the work of implementation begins.

- *We don't want to be (or listen to) a naysayer.* We all know people who can see only the problems in things—never the opportunities. Addressing their fears and concerns can be exhausting. On the other hand, when everyone seems excited about a decision, or just relieved a decision was made, raising negative issues is difficult.

- *We know situations are unpredictable.* We accept as a given the fact that the future is uncertain. Because of our inability to perfectly predict what may happen, not to try at all is easier. Consequently, we sometimes ignore factors that could be anticipated, just because we can't be sure of everything.

- *We have confidence in our conclusions.* By the time we make a big decision, we probably feel we know a situation well. Because of our confidence in the choice, we may believe that examining how to implement the decision most effectively is unimportant. We are tempted to think that because a choice is "right," no problems will occur. As we know, however, that situation is rarely the case.

- *We face competing priorities.* We often juggle multiple priorities. Once one issue is resolved (i.e., something decided), some other issue begs our attention. Sometimes we see planning for successful implementation as taking us away from another pressing concern. Because the future hasn't happened, we find it is easy to race to the next task and hope for the best.

• *We know firefighting is rewarded.* Often we want to feel vital and important and busy. We all know people who race around putting out proverbial fires and running from one problem to another. Their frenetic activity and the fact that others come to them for help make them look heroic, important, and pivotal to an operation. Yet how many of those fires could have been prevented? Planning is sometimes a silent activity. Measuring the problems we prevent is not easy. It is far easier to measure how quickly we were able to respond or address a problem once it occurred. Therefore, we tend to reward firefighting over fire prevention.

Once a goal has been set, we need to decide how best to achieve that goal. When we choose an alternative, prepare to implement a change, or take an action, we are going to change the future in some way. Our success in achieving a goal or making a change is influenced by how effectively we address obstacles that may get in the way. Potential problem analysis allows us to anticipate factors that may impede our progress so we can either prevent them or minimize their consequences. We can use potential problem analysis any time we need to successfully make a change, take an action, implement a decision, or achieve a goal. In short, we use potential problem analysis when we need to ensure future success.

A Scenario for Potential Problem Analysis

Over the last year, district and school leaders in a school district have experienced increasing pressure to address issues related to high school students who leave campus at lunchtime. Nearby residents complain that students litter and cut through their property on the way to a local sandwich shop. Many students in this affluent community drive to school. Teachers report that students often miss or arrive late for the class period after lunch. Several students have been arrested during lunchtime for driving under the influence. The whole matter reached a crisis last week when two students were involved in a serious accident shortly after lunch. Their blood-alcohol level was twice the legal limit.

In the face of mounting pressure to take action, the district has decided to close the high school campus during lunch. Students will not be allowed to leave campus during lunch periods without special written permission signed by their parents. The decision is controversial, but the school board believes that this solution is the best way in the short term to manage the situation and let the parents and the community know it is taking the matter seriously and is responding sensibly.

Structure of a Potential Problem

Before discussing the scenario within the context of the steps of potential problem analysis, we first need to look at the structure of a potential problem. Potential problems have causes, and they create effects. Because we are looking into the future, however, and are not sure what problems will arise or what the causes and effects might be, we use language that reflects this uncertainty. *Likely causes* create *potential problems*. These problems, in turn, have *potential effects*. For example, if we plan a vacation, we might worry about missing our airplane flight. Some likely causes for this potential problem might be not leaving enough time to get to the airport, getting lost on the way to the airport, or getting caught in traffic. If we miss our flight, effects include being stranded at the airport, having to find another flight, having to spend more money to change our flight, and (in a worst case scenario) having to cancel our vacation.

Potential problem analysis helps us identify two different kinds of actions we can take to address potential problems. We take *preventive actions* to prevent the problem from occurring. If the problem does occur, *contingent actions* help minimize its effects. Typically, the payoff for preventing problems is greater than the payoff for dealing with them after they occur. Sometimes problems occur despite our best efforts at prevention. We need to be prepared to respond. Figure 4.1 shows how our responses correspond to the elements of a potential problem.

The Steps in Potential Problem Analysis

The acronym PLAN allows us to focus on the primary purpose of potential problem analysis. Each letter in the acronym stands for a different step (shown earlier in Figure 1.4):

- **P**redict potential problems.
- **L**ist likely causes.
- **A**gree on preventive actions.
- **N**ote contingent actions.

In this section, we examine each step in the potential problem analysis process and look at how it might apply in an actual situation. We discuss the key questions the step is designed to

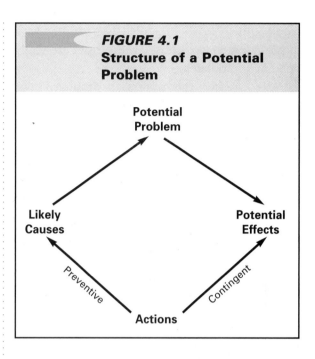

FIGURE 4.1
Structure of a Potential Problem

Potential Problem

Likely Causes

Potential Effects

Preventive

Contingent

Actions

answer and the purpose for each step. Then we look at how the step applies to the decision to close the high school campus (the scenario given earlier in the chapter). Remember that potential problem analysis does not apply until we decide that we need to take some action, such as implement a decision, change something, or plan.

Predict Potential Problems

This step answers the key questions, What could go wrong? What problems could arise? Often we don't want to think about what might go wrong; such thoughts can be scary or overwhelming. But choosing not to look at potential problems does not eliminate them. Rather, if we are prepared, we have power.

We need to use our experience to determine what problems might arise and ask others about their experience in similar situations. If we have completed a decision analysis, we can look at the risks we identified as associated with the alternative we chose. These risks are really potential problems.

In stating the potential problems, we should be as specific as possible. The more nebulous our potential problems, the harder it is to identify effective actions. For example, if in planning our vacation, we stated a potential problem as money, what would that mean? It could mean not having enough money, not knowing how to use or convert foreign money, or losing money on the trip. When we restate the problem as running out of money, we can be more specific in determining how to handle the problem.

Potential problems frequently arise in the following situations:

- We are doing something for the first time.
- We have tight deadlines.
- Several people, systems, or departments have overlapping responsibility or authority.
- We need help or support from others outside our direct influence.
- We require extensive interaction or cooperation from multiple people or groups of people.
- We are dealing with problems that have a high visibility or widespread effect.

Applying the Process:
Closed-Campus Example

The decision has been made to close the high school campus during lunch hour for students in grades 9 through 12, starting in September with the beginning of the school year. The challenge is to implement that decision as effectively as possible. A task force interviews various stakeholders, such as students, parents, school administrators, teachers, and cafeteria personnel, to identify issues and potential problems that might arise. Based on this input, task force members develop a list of potential problems:

- Angry students leaving the campus en masse.*
- Inability to feed all students during lunch hour.*
- Inadequate staff support for a closed campus.
- Insufficient food varieties.
- Inadequate supervision.*
- Increased student conflicts at noon.
- Handling special student and parent requests to be off campus at noon.

*High-priority items.

The task force begins by looking at potential problems it deems most serious and likely to occur (indicated by an asterisk [*]). These high-priority problems are listed in Figure. 4.2 (p. 58).

List Likely Causes

In this step, we examine each potential problem and ask, What could cause this problem to occur? A problem might have several different causes. Because we do not know what might actually create the problem, we want to have the opportunity to address each of the likely causes.

Applying the Process:
Closed-Campus Example

The task force focuses on the three main problems and identifies the most likely causes of each problem (see Figure 4.2).

Agree on Preventive Actions

Once we know what could go wrong, we look at how to prevent problems. We take each likely cause and ask, What can we do to keep this likely cause from occurring or from creating the potential problem?

In this step, we identify actions we can take to prevent the potential problem from occurring. We look at multiple causes because we don't know which, if any, cause will create the problem. By addressing each likely cause, we decrease the probability that the problem will occur, and we maximize the probability that we will prevent the problem.

When we try to determine what preventive actions to take, we need to consider factors such as cost, ease of implementation, and potential effectiveness. When we can identify several possible preventive actions, considering these factors helps us narrow down which actions to take.

Applying the Process:
Closed-Campus Example

The task force develops preventive actions that the school can take (see Figure 4.2) after talking with food service staff, building administrators, students, and others for ideas about what they can do to prevent the likely causes and potential problems from occurring.

Note Contingent Actions

Sometimes, despite our best efforts at prevention, the problem occurs anyway. In that event, we want to be prepared to take effective action. We don't want to wait until the problem occurs to figure out how to handle it, so we plan ahead.

For each potential problem we ask, What can we do if the potential problem occurs? Because contingent actions help minimize the damage a problem creates, the timing of those contingent actions is important. Typically, the more quickly we take action, the less the damage will be. Therefore, we should plan these actions in advance and not wait until a problem occurs. For example, if we miss our airplane yet know exactly what our backup plan is (i.e., which alternate flight to take), we spend less time trying to find another flight and more time on the beach!

Applying the Process:
Closed-Campus Example

Task force members hope that the good ideas others have provided about how to prevent the problems will work. But they need to be prepared in case the problems arise anyway. So they look at each potential problem and consider what actions they should take if the problem occurs. For example, with the first problem, they ask, What should be done if we find we can't feed all the students during the designated lunch period? By asking others and brainstorming, they identify viable contingent actions, shown in Figure 4.2.

What Do We Do with the Actions We've Identified?

Of course, all the good work we have put into our analysis is of no avail if we don't take action. We need to implement the preventive and

FIGURE 4.2
Applying Potential Problem Analysis in the Closed-Campus Example

Potential Problem	Likely Causes	Preventive Actions	Contingent Actions
Inability to feed all students during lunch hour	Not enough food.	Social pressure. Have additional food carts available.	Extend lunch period.
	Slow lines.	Have dry run for staff and students.	
	Limited space.	Designate other supervised lunch areas.	
Inadequate supervision	Too many exits.	Close as many exit doors as possible.	Install a video camera.
	Lack of volunteer supervisors.	Provide free lunch for volunteers.	Call district office for backup.
Angry students leaving the campus en masse	Sense of feeling controlled and betrayed.	Provide clear communication; meet with student leaders.	Give reprimand notes to students who leave.
	Limited choice of food options.	Arrange for a variety of food carts.	Restrict access upon return.
		Ask student leaders to write letters.	Notify parents.

contingent actions we've identified. If we have developed a step-by-step action plan for implementing whatever we are trying to accomplish, we can integrate these actions into the plan, making them additional steps. In the absence of some plan, we consider these questions: Who will be responsible for implementing each preventive action? What do they need to do? By when?

For contingent actions, what needs to be done in advance to ensure that the contingent actions are ready (in the event the potential problem occurs)? How will we know the problem has occurred? Who will be responsible for taking the contingent action?

Potential *Opportunity* Analysis

As hard as it can be for us to think proactively to prevent problems, it is even harder to think about the opportunities we might create when we decide to make some change. The same logic applies, though. Rather than trying to prevent potential problems, we are trying to create *potential opportunities*. These opportunities have *likely causes*. Because we want to create or encourage these causes, we develop *promoting actions*. Once the potential opportunity occurs, we want to make the most of it, so we plan *exploiting* or *capitalizing actions*.

For example, a staff unit decides to invest in a certain kind of training. To make the most of their investment, they apply potential opportunity analysis. Figure 4.3 (p. 60) shows a matrix they used to help them maximize the effectiveness of the training.

Applying Potential Problem Analysis in Schools

Let's examine situations where administrators and teachers found potential problem analysis useful. First, we look at how potential problem analysis has been used in administrative settings, and then we look at how it has been used with and by students.

Examples of Administrative Use

Dealing with unexpected change. El Morro Elementary School (Laguna Beach, California) experienced an unexpected increase in kindergarten enrollment. A team of school staff and teachers examined the situation and considered seven possible options. Team members finally decided the best way to handle the increase was to create an additional kindergarten classroom. The merits of this choice were that it would result in a lower kindergarten student-to-teacher ratio, strengthen the early reading literacy program, and eliminate all combination classrooms. It did, however, carry some risks: It would require student movement at three grade levels (K–2) and would result in a higher student-to-teacher ratio in 1st and 2nd grades. The team identified several potential problems:

- Lack of parental understanding and acceptance of the decision.
- Failure to disseminate information in a consistent and timely manner.
- Inability to secure sufficient instructional aide support for 2nd grade.
- Lack of an appropriate location for the additional kindergarten class.
- Inability to determine the appropriate composition of kindergarten, 1st, and 2nd grade classes.

Let's look more closely at how they applied potential problem analysis to one particular high-threat potential problem: lack of parental understanding and acceptance of the decision. Here is what the team identified:

- *Likely causes*
  - Information is leaked early.
  - Parents are unclear about extent of the problem.
  - Staff is not applying the personal touch when communicating with parents whose children are involved.
  - Information is sent out late.

- *Preventive actions*
  - School sends parents an awareness letter explaining reasoning and the decision-making process.
  - Teachers make personal phone calls to the parents and students who are involved.

FIGURE 4.3
Using Potential Opportunity Analysis to Maximize Training Effectiveness

Potential Opportunity *What do we want to happen?*	Likely Causes *What would cause the potential opportunity?*	Promoting Actions *What could we do to create a likely cause?*	Exploiting Actions *Once we have greater exposure, what can we do to make the most of it?*
Staff awareness to be enhanced	Hold a three-day workshop with staff.	Schedule the workshop.	Share products beyond our department.
	Discuss at staff meetings.	Include discussion and form in agendas.	
	Use the training concept with staff.	Use the process with staff.	
Staff to become "users"	Recognize when we can use training concepts.	Make a commitment to find opportunities to use them.	Assist and coach others beyond our unit.
	Apply training concepts to issues.	Seek a coach and support from each other.	
	Purposely plan to use training concepts.	Use training concept vocabulary.	
		Provide a template for each process.	
Staff to model the process	Observe others using the concepts and share observations.	Practice with a coach (all participants).	Use tools when assisting other departments.
	Feel successful using the concepts; see success and *share*.	Accept feedback.	

○ School sends second personalized letter to the same parents.

○ School gives parents the opportunity to meet the new teacher during November parent conferences.

Recognizing that, despite the preventive measures, parents may still be upset, the school's contingency plan is for teachers to record the level of parental acceptance during communications. If parental acceptance is high, no further action is needed. If the level of acceptance is low, teachers will schedule a meeting with parents to address concerns.

Planning a meeting. Members of a task force, preparing to present recommendations to all school teachers and administrators, were nervous about how their recommendations would be received. There had been a lot of heated debate about this issue. The task force had spent up-front time investigating the issue properly and was confident it had made the right choice. Team members used potential problem analysis to plan for this critical meeting. Figure 4.4 (p. 62) shows part of their analysis.

Action planning. Orange County Public School District (Orlando, Florida) was considering whether to implement a new standardized guidance program throughout the district. Task force members used potential problem analysis to identify the primary potential problems they faced and the likely causes. Once they had identified these potential problems, they saw a range of ways they hadn't considered to prevent the problems. Members also made sure they had some contingent actions in place. Then they developed an action plan for next steps. For each action (preventive or contingent), they identified a person or team to be responsible for that action and the date by which the action should be taken.

Using others to help identify potential problems. A high school in New Jersey prepared to implement a controversial strict no-smoking policy. The school administration met with groups of stakeholders (e.g., students, parents, teachers, staff, and law enforcement officials) to get a sense of the issues and concerns they had about the new policy. The administra-

tive team found that many of the issues were really potential problems:

- Smokers are unable to quit smoking during the day.
- Students leave campus just to smoke.
- Administrators cannot enforce the policy.
- Smokers feel victimized and persecuted.

After they had identified potential problems, administrators applied the rest of the process to identify preventive and contingent actions to deal with the problems.

Examples of Classroom Use

Teachers may use potential problem analysis to help students stretch their thinking about curriculum material. Students might analyze actions or changes that others had decided to make. What potential problems did others not consider? What preventive and contingent actions did others take? What consequences might have been avoided had they done a little planning? Teachers may help students apply these skills in other situations (e.g., planning a team project or student activity) as well. The following examples from real schools illustrate the potential for using potential problem analysis to enhance the curriculum.

Relating to a current issue. At George Washington Middle School (Alexandria, Virginia), students are studying Census 2000. Their social studies teacher asks them to fill out an actual census form, visit the census Web site to read frequently asked questions, and read a short article that talks about a dilemma multiracial families face when they fill out the form. Here's the dilemma: What box or boxes should a multiracial family check to denote the family's

---

FIGURE 4.4
Using Potential Problem Analysis to Plan for a Difficult Meeting

Potential Problem	Likely Causes	Preventive Actions	Contingent Actions
Inability to adequately handle negative feedback	Staff doesn't want change.	Be prepared—recognizing we are all in a different place.	Ask people to write down concerns for presenters to review and respond to later.
	Staff fears change.	Explain what the benefits are to students and staff; indicate support is available; reassure staff that signing up indicates only studying an area.	
	Presenters start to become defensive.	During presentation, explain that all types of questions are welcome.	
Lack of full staff participation	Staff is uninterested.	Indicate that this activity is a precursor to a staff development day.	Talk with people one-on-one.
	Staff is apathetic.	Have everyone complete a questionnaire (anonymously).	
Inability to complete all defined tasks during the one-hour meeting	Addressing questions takes too much time.	Write down questions.	Carry discussion over to another staff meeting.
	Presentations take too long.	Limit time for each sequence; ask staff to hold questions until the presentation is finished.	

---

ethnicity? Some demographic groups are urging multiracial individuals to choose only one box; others are urging people to choose all boxes that apply. The teacher gives students one potential problem to consider: People may not fill out the form, then federal funding for schools and other community programs might not get to multiracial communities.

Students consider some likely causes for multiracial families not filling out the form:

• Form is too long.

• Form has 63 different multiracial combinations.

• Participants think they may check only one box.

• Form has insufficient information on how to fill it out.

• People think the form is junk mail.

• People believe the form is another government form too close to tax deadlines.

Students next consider what preventive and contingent actions they could take to address the potential problem. Here are some preventive actions they identified:

• Provide a shorter form.

• Include more publicity on how to fill out the form.

• Make more boxes for multiracial people.

• Hold free community information sessions.

• Conduct census at a different time of year.

The teacher reports a benefit of this exercise: It fosters creative thinking about actions, specifically, how to address problems. The children can also now recognize situations outside class where potential problem analysis applies (e.g., having to leave early for athletics, doing group work, and trying to juggle multiple student activities). These are situations in which students have to think ahead, and they see the value of preparation. About three weeks after this exercise, the media produced a lot of coverage about problems related to the census. Students approached the teacher, pointing out that the class had predicted some of these problems. The media coverage validated some of their effort. The class is also racially diverse and includes many multiracial children. Children of

mixed race wrestle with the issue of racial identification and were able to see how many others struggle with the same issues. Their frame of reference added a new dimension to the discussion.

Digging more deeply into an issue. At John Witherspoon Middle School (Princeton, New Jersey), 7th grade science students are studying geologic time and fossils. They read a newspaper article about a group of scientists who want to thaw a male woolly mammoth and retrieve its DNA so that this extinct mammal can possibly be cloned. At first, the students make statements like, "It won't work," or "It's too dangerous so the scientists shouldn't do it." Their responses are gut reaction. The teacher's further probing indicates that their conclusions lack clarity and supporting rationale. Then the teacher has the students apply the steps of potential problem analysis. In Figure 4.5 (p. 64), we see an example of some students' analyses.

Although many potential problems exist, the students can identify ways to handle them through possible preventive and contingent actions. The teacher notes that potential problem analysis forces students to delve more deeply into an issue, not just skim the surface. Specifically, the tool helps them organize their thinking and exploration while it requires them to support conclusions with evidence. Potential problem analysis also helps them use deductive reasoning to predict causes of potential problems and then develop plans of action to address them. Such skills are required for good scientific thinking.

Tackling tough issues. A team of peer counselors (students who mentor their peers) at Laguna Beach High School (Laguna Beach, California) is using potential problem analysis

FIGURE 4.5
Using Potential Problem Analysis to Plan Thawing a Woolly Mammoth

Step 1: Predict Potential Problems *What could go wrong?*	Step 2: Likely Causes *What could be the cause of these problems?*	Step 3: Agree on Preventive Actions *What can you do to avoid the cause of these problems?*	Step 4: Note Contingent Actions *What's your backup plan if problems still occur?*
DNA may not be usable.	DNA is not kept cold enough.	Refreeze DNA artificially and hope that it can be used.	Save the male's DNA for the future.
Cloned mammoth would not be an identical mammoth clone. It would be a cross between an elephant and a mammoth—a semiclone.	No female mammoth, which is needed for DNA sample, has been found, so an elephant must provide female DNA.	Continue to look for a preserved female mammoth.	Accept that this semiclone is fairly close. Be prepared to kill the clone.
If cloning works, mammoth may not have proper or enough food.	Natural food is no longer available; what mammoth really eats or how much is unknown.	Look for frozen food and clone it, too; if it cannot be found, feed the mammoth food that elephants eat and alter the diet whenever appropriate.	Do not clone the mammoth but keep it in a special cold museum for people to view (finding the mammoth is incredible enough, even without cloning it).
Environment is not the same, so clone may die.	Because the Ice Age occurred a long time ago, we are not totally sure what a mammoth's environment was like, plus our time has new and different diseases.	Create an artificial biodome to house the mammoth.	
Cloned mammoth escapes and causes harm to ecosystem or other animals and plants.	It is a "new" species in a "new" environment, with unknown effects.	Watch mammoth carefully, using a setting where it is away from many humans and other animals.	
Major ethical issues with introducing "new" species arise.	People's concern is, are we trying to play God?	Try to explain to people that this mammoth could help scientists better understand the past.	

to investigate potential problems that their mentoring program for students might have to deal with. One potential problem for mentorees is having a confrontation with a teacher. The student counselors interview students and teachers to find out what might cause these confrontations. Teachers relate problems such as "constant misbehavior," "not having respect for peers," and "not telling the truth." Students say the most likely causes are that "teachers are in a bad mood" or "teachers don't like certain students." When the counselors present their findings to the students and staff, each group denies that those likely causes apply to them. The student counselors then create a scenario where a student is thrown out of class for talking too much. Teams of students and staff brainstorm likely causes for this event. Their responses include answers such as "class is not interesting," "student is distracted by issues outside of class," and "student needs clarification."

Without going any further than identifying potential problems and likely causes, each group of stakeholders was able to gain greater appreciation of the other group's perspective. The session ended with staff having greater appreciation for the pressures that students face and for the reasons that students might react the way some do. Students realized some of the staff's rationale for handling difficult situations.

Spurring creativity. Middle school science students at Maitland Middle School (Maitland, Florida) are studying earthquakes. Through reading and discussion, they have identified several potential problems, such as fires and explosions, buildings falling down, flooding, and destruction of utilities. Because they are clear about the potential problems and likely causes, students are free to be innovative and imaginative in identifying possible preventive and contingent actions. Figure 4.6 (p. 66) shows student work to identify likely causes, preventive actions, and contingent actions for the potential problem of fires and explosions from an earthquake. These actions can then be more closely examined for feasibility. Where necessary, the activity allows the teacher to help students see when their thinking is based on misconceptions or faulty logic.

Other student-related examples. Below are more examples of using potential problem analysis with students:

• The novel *Catcher in the Rye* ends with Holden Caulfield about to return home after staying in a mental institution. High school students examine some of the potential problems he faces, such as not doing well in school, not getting along with his parents, being unhappy, and hurting himself. They draw from the book to identify future problems and causes, based on Holden's experiences. Then they identify actions Holden, his parents, and others can take to keep these problems from arising. This exercise not only deepens the students' appreciation of the book, but also raises issues relevant to their own lives.

• A high-school economics class examines the problems that can arise when a country adopts a new economic or government system. They look at moving from Marxism to capitalism and some of the implications (e.g., potential problems and their likely causes) of that change. When students develop preventive and contingent actions to address these potential problems, they see the motivation behind some of the actions that governments have taken when they made this transition.

FIGURE 4.6
Addressing the Potential Problem of Fires and Explosions from Earthquakes

Likely Cause	Preventive Actions	Contingent Actions
Gas leaks	Use many-layered tubes and pipes.	Have controls to shut off gas when necessary.
	Use rubber tubes and pipes.	Have water tower on top of buildings and release water if fire breaks out.
	Don't use gas; use electricity.	Put important records in fireproof buildings.
		Specify an evacuation route.
Falling power lines	Put power lines underground.	
	Make poles flexible but strong.	
Falling buildings	Secure buildings to ground.	
	Have automatic shutdown of utilities for emergencies.	

• A middle school science class in Laguna Beach, California, prepares to revegetate the canyons that have been burned in recent fires. They apply their knowledge of propagation, flora, fauna, and environmental conditions to identify potential problems they might face and ways to handle them.

• A physical education teacher helps students anticipate the potential problems of sticking to a new exercise plan. Students identify preventive actions that will help them achieve and maintain their exercise goals.

• Social studies students at Whitman Middle School (Wauwatosa, Wisconsin) are studying a unit on westward expansion. Students are to imagine that they are preparing to emigrate to the West. They determine what potential problems they face, how to prevent those problems, and what to do if the problems occur. The students see how these problems influence such considerations as the routes they choose, the provisions they take, the people they take with them, and their methods of transport.

• Elementary school students prepare for a class trip. Their teacher asks them to think about what could go wrong (e.g., someone could get lost), and together they develop simple actions that can keep those things from happening. Students appreciate more the need for some of the rules for the trip because they've helped develop them.

Potential problem analysis helps us maximize the chance of achieving our goals by helping remove or address obstacles that may get in our way. Proactive planning helps school administrators, teachers, and students minimize some of the anxiety that change and uncertainty can bring. When we use potential problem analysis in the curriculum, we learn from the way others have handled change, and we better understand how, by a little foresight and ingenuity, we can reap rewards. This process requires and reinforces a deeper understanding of the subject matter.

< 5 >

Problem Analysis:
Why Did This Happen?
Solving Problems by Finding True Cause

A problem well defined is half-solved.

—ARISTOTLE

Most of us in education can remember at least one (and, unfortunately, probably more than one) situation where things went unexpectedly wrong: Schoolwide test scores came back lower than expected, teachers left for other districts, and the number of threatening incidents involving students increased from last year. When things go wrong, we often act in predictable ways. As the effects of a problem become more widespread and severe, our anxiety increases. As anxiety increases, we revert to our favorite coping mechanisms:

• *Jumping to a cause.* When something goes wrong, we often theorize about what happened. We believe we know why the problem occurred; everyone else also seems to be an expert on what the problem is and how to fix it. Maybe we have seen the problem before, or it seems similar to another situation. The more we advocate for a particular cause, the more invested we become in proving that this cause is the root of the problem. We use data to support our theory (and ignore other data that refute it). We tinker and make adjustments or changes to fix the problem.

• *Fixing blame.* For some reason, our first tendency is often to determine who's at fault. We point fingers at each other, rather than address the problem. This behavior immediately creates defensiveness and erects barriers that are counterproductive to cooperative problem solving.

• *Taking ineffective action.* To do *something*, we begin to propose solutions and make adjustments, hoping these changes will make things better. Although we often must take quick action in the face of a problem, those actions don't always eliminate the problem. They may or may not minimize the damage. We feel better, however, if we take some kind of action; at least we're trying. We feel as if others are saying, "Don't just stand there—do something." Unfortunately, these quick actions can be ineffective and, at worst, may create more problems than they solve.

• *Suffering analysis paralysis.* We might *want* first to investigate and gather data; we just don't seem to know when to stop. Learning more about a problem before we make sweeping changes makes sense, but sometimes we avoid taking action by continuing to collect data.

• *Using selective data.* We may ignore information relevant to the problem or use selected facts to bolster our own theories. Using selective data prevents us from recognizing relevant facts about a problem and understanding its true nature. It may also cause us to act using faulty reasoning.

Problems result from cause-and-effect sequencing. Something creates effects that are abnormal or difficult to live with. For example, if your home's heat goes out, you will likely become aware of the problem when you begin to feel the effects—a cold house.

When something goes wrong, we can take two main types of actions: Band-Aid actions that deal with effects, or corrective actions that address cause. If our heat isn't working properly, we can put on a sweater or plug in a space heater. These actions deal with the effects, and they may help us feel warmer—for a while. We might also adjust the thermostat or clean the fil-

ters. We don't know, however, if we have solved the problem unless we know what *caused* the problem. Sometimes we take some action, and the problem seems to go away; we believe we've fixed it. But the problem reappears. Only actions that address the true cause of the problem will fix that problem. Figure 5.1 shows the correlation between these possible problem-solving actions and the structure of a problem.

Have you ever seen a problem that gets fixed again and again, but never really goes away? That phenomenon occurs when we throw actions at the problem's effects without understanding the problem's cause. For example, to raise reading levels, a school district launches a new reading program. After the first year, teachers complain bitterly about the program, and student reading scores show no improvement. The district provides additional training. The teachers decide to make adjustments in the program. A task force contacts the vendor for suggested improvements. Frustration during the second year is still high.

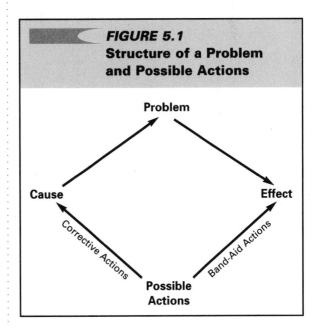

FIGURE 5.1
Structure of a Problem and Possible Actions

When the reading scores come in, the program is scrapped. A new reading program is launched in the third year with just as much fanfare and hope. Another initiative bites the proverbial dust. Rather than addressing the complicated causes of the low reading scores, we pin our hopes on another Band-Aid solution.

In other instances, these Band-Aid actions can be successful enough to make us feel less pain and even feel as though we have fixed the problem. What if reading scores had actually risen? It would be easy to attribute the rise to the new program, although the new program may or may not be responsible. Such a result is why problem solving often stops if some improvement occurs.

The only way to really *eliminate* a problem is to take action that is aimed at the cause. Band-Aid actions are still often necessary. They can mitigate damage and buy time while we investigate. Such actions function much like triage, when medical personnel assess damage and take measures to stop the bleeding until the problem can be adequately addressed. In problem solving, these actions buy us time while we find the cause. We often think we don't have time to do more than make the problem go away—for now. But have you ever noticed we have time to address the same problem again and again? Why not fix it right the first time? Finding the cause and taking appropriate action to eliminate it allows us to solve the problem. Problem analysis is a tool to help us gather and organize information to determine the cause of a problem.

When to Use Problem Analysis

When people say they have a problem, they may be referring to many different types of situa-tions. We use problem analysis only in situations that meet three specific conditions:

- *A deviation exists between what should happen and what actually happens.* A performance of some kind is different from what it should be. Perhaps attendance is down, teacher turnover is up, or test scores have fallen. The clearer we are about what our expectations are (the *should*) and the more we know about what is actually happening (the *actual*), the more quickly and clearly we can identify and address deviations.

- *We do not know the cause.* Because problem analysis is a cause-finding tool, we do not apply it when we already know what has caused the deviation.

- *We need to know the cause to take effective action.* Sometimes we do not need to know the cause to take effective action. If the caterer is late with the food for the banquet, for example, we know we have a deviation; we do not know why. But to take action, we don't need to know why. We just want to find out when the caterers will arrive and find other food to tide people over until then.

A Scenario for Problem Analysis

It is mid-May and a meeting is in progress at Fairmont Middle School. Present are Dr. Sarah Morris, principal; Mr. James Blackwell, assistant principal; and Ms. Kimberly Testa, math lab teacher. They are meeting to discuss the future of their math computer lab. Recently, staff have been asking questions about its efficacy in augmenting student skills. Budget cuts are forcing everyone to examine programs more closely. Here's the discussion:

Dr. Morris: Kimberly, there is no question that some students are being helped by your work in the lab. However, many other students seem to be making little or no progress. You know we are losing some funding, and we cannot afford to offer services that do not have a positive result. That is not to say we are cutting your program. We just need to look more closely at it, just as we are looking at many other programs. No matter what, we need to determine how to make your program even more effective.

Ms. Testa: Dr. Morris, I appreciate the position you are in. But with the most recent results showing how poorly our students are doing in math, I just don't see why this program would be cut. I believe we should put *more* resources into this program, not fewer.

Mr. Blackwell: Actually, those same test results seem to be turning up the heat around this program. I've received a number of calls from angry parents who wonder why their children did so badly on the tests. The students spend time in the lab, yet they don't seem to have anything to show for it. Several parents mentioned the big deal we made last year when we opened the lab, about how it would help better prepare our students.

Dr. Morris: Of course, who knows how badly the students would have done without the lab. Results might have been a whole lot worse.

Ms. Testa: That's exactly what I've been saying. For every negative parent comment, I have a positive student or teacher comment saying what a difference the lab makes for them. I feel that everyone blames us, and nobody recognizes the value we add. Why isn't anyone scrutinizing the math teachers and curriculum?

Mr. Blackwell: We are looking at those things, too, but this meeting is to talk about the math lab and what we can do to improve it.

Ms. Testa: Well, there is only so much my team and I can do. You know these students' abilities are already lagging when they get to school. They are several steps behind before they even start. And they don't get much help from their parents. I know the math teachers are working hard, but I have real doubts about the efficacy of their methods. Then these students show up at the lab and we're expected to perform miracles.

Dr. Morris: No one is expecting a miracle. We just want to be sure what we're doing is working. Have you tried using the new learning software or presenting activities to make learning fun? What about changing the time that lab is offered? How do you feel about the results you see from students in your lab?

Ms. Testa: Well, some students are making good progress. But I would have to agree that other students are making little or no progress. I don't understand that, because we have taken several actions over the past year to boost performance. We have installed new software, applied games to make learning fun, and improved the room layout. We thought these things would all help. Now I'm not sure they did.

Mr. Blackwell: I would like to use this as an opportunity to try problem analysis to find the cause for this problem. Would that be okay with you, Kimberly?

Ms. Testa: Okay. It would be good to get to the bottom of this. Let me know what I can do to help.

The scenario illustrates some factors that make problem solving difficult:

- Participants have insufficient meaningful data or information, or data are being used inefficiently. Typically, information must be gleaned from a variety of sources.
- Stakeholders may get defensive and feel under attack.
- Participants brainstorm possible solutions before they understand why the problem exists.
- No one person has all the data.

The Steps in Problem Analysis

Problem analysis helps us gather, sort, organize, and analyze relevant data to identify the true cause of a problem. Like the other analytic processes, problem analysis comprises a set of sequenced questions. We use the acronym FIND to describe the steps of the problem analysis process. Each letter in the acronym stands for a key problem-solving step (shown earlier in Figure 1.4):

- **F**ocus on the problem.
- **I**dentify what *is* and *is not*.
- **N**arrow possible causes.
- **D**etermine the true cause.

In this section, we examine each step and show how it applies to the scenario given earlier.

Focus on the Problem

In the first step, we clearly state the problem we are working on. Often, several problems need attention, and sometimes they overlap. We need to identify the specific deviation we examine. This step answers the key question, What specific problem needs to be solved? We write a simple statement that includes an *object* (the thing, the group of things, or the person or people that have the problem) and the *defect* (what is wrong). We check our problem statement to ensure we have an object and defect and we are dealing with a cause-unknown deviation.

Applying the Process: Math Lab Example

Although a couple of problems are mentioned in the scenario (e.g., students not progressing in lab and low student math scores), we look only at the problem directly involving the math lab.

Mr. Blackwell states the problem as, Math lab students are not progressing. The objects (or people) in this problem are math lab students. The observable defect is, They are not progressing. Use these questions to determine if this statement and situation meet the three conditions for applying problem analysis:

- *Does a deviation exist between what should happen and what actually happens?* Yes. Clearly, students are supposed to be making progress with their math skills within the lab. Some discrepancy is obvious in opinions about how big a problem that lack of progress is, but even the math lab teacher admits a problem does exist.
- *Do we know the cause?* No. We do not know why there is a lack of progress. Several theories are put forward, but no definitive answer appears.
- *Do we need to know the cause to take effective action?* Yes. Knowing the cause helps us take action aimed more directly at the root of the problem. Ms. Testa mentioned several actions already taken to improve student progress. Apparently, they had little or no effect.

This situation is a good candidate for problem analysis. But what if Mr. Blackwell had stated the problem as, Parents are upset? Problem analysis would not apply because we already know the cause—the parents are upset because of their children's math scores and the apparent ineffectiveness of the lab. We use problem analysis to find the cause. The problem statement should present a problem for which the cause is unknown. We need to find out why the math lab students aren't progressing.

Identify What *Is* and *Is Not*

Before we can determine what caused a problem, we need to better understand the problem. In this step, we gather specific information about a problem and its effects to build a complete description of it. Information helps us form a clearer picture, or description, of the situation. In turn, this description suggests possible causes and helps us test their viability. To better understand the problem, we ask specific questions in four areas:

- What is the *identity* of the deviation we are describing?
- Where is the *location* of the deviation?
- When is the *timing* of the deviation?
- To what extent is the *magnitude* of the deviation?

For each area, we ask two different types of questions: those that relate to what the problem *is* and those that relate to what the problem *is not*. The *is not* questions look at factors that might logically be involved but are not (the closest logical comparison). The *is not* questions give us an even more complete picture of the problem. These questions help us tighten our description of the problem and provide us with a basis of comparison from which to draw conclusions. Figure 5.2 (p. 75) shows the complete set of *is* and *is not* questions we ask in the four areas.

The concept of the *is not* at first may seem strange. *Is* and *is not* thinking, however, come naturally to most of us. Imagine you are watching your favorite television program and the picture goes fuzzy. What is the first thing you do? Perhaps you check what is happening on other channels. If they are fuzzy, you might try another television in your house to see if the same problem exists. If that television is fuzzy, maybe you call a neighbor to see if they have the same problem, or you call the cable TV company. You are trying to put boundaries around the problem, to see where it *is* and where it *is not*. Why? You know that if one television is fuzzy and the other television is fine, chances are, the cause of the problem lies within your one television, not with the cable TV company.

The 11 pairs of *is* and *is not* questions help us clearly and thoroughly define the problem we are dealing with. They help us identify and display relevant data meaningfully. Not every question will apply to every situation. You can always disregard questions that don't seem to apply. How would these questions apply to our math lab scenario? Figure 5.3 (p. 76) shows Mr. Blackwell's answers to the questions. We call such information a completed problem specification—we have specified the relevant facts about the deviation.

Applying the Process: Math Lab Example

As you can see, the *is* and *is not* questions are worded generically so they can be applied to any scenario. The questions may seem awkward at first, but when we understand the kind of information each question seeks, we can modify the questions according to the situation. Let's look at how Mr. Blackwell uses the questions in the math lab example:

• *What* questions. These questions focus on identifying the specific object (or people) we are having a problem with and the specific defect. The corresponding *is not* questions look at what people or defects you might expect to see but don't. We know from our problem statement that our object is math lab students. We can be more specific by asking, Which math lab students? When Mr. Blackwell asks more specific questions, he finds the 7th and 8th grade students are primarily the ones who are not progressing. The 5th and 6th grade students seem to be progressing well.

Earlier in the chapter, we identified the defect as, They are not progressing. Mr. Blackwell asks Ms. Testa to be more specific about what "not progressing" means. She says there has been minimal improvement over entering scores. She identifies other kinds of problems she might expect but isn't seeing (e.g., high absenteeism and disruptive behavior).

• *Where* questions. The problem is observed in the math lab. The teachers of these 7th and 8th grade students report that even though test results are disappointing, the students make good progress during class. The students handle the homework and in-class work well.

The second pair of *where* questions does not apply to this situation, so we write N/A.

• *When* questions. Mr. Blackwell collects information showing that the problem first became evident after the winter break (starting January 5, 2000). Since then, it has been a continuous problem; there is no pattern or periodicity. In addition, the problem is not sporadic. Almost all 7th and 8th grade students have made little progress on their scores since the beginning of January.

The third pair of *when* questions deals with life cycle. This pair looks at the stages someone or something moves through, to see if some correlation exists between what an object is doing, what is being done to an object, and when the problem occurs. If we have problems with a car stalling, we might look at the life cycle of operating our car: starting the car, putting it in gear, accelerating, idling, decelerating, and so forth. If the car stalls only when it's idling and not during acceleration, that might provide important clues about what causes the car to stall. In the math lab example, we might look at the stages in the student calendar. The problem was first observed right after winter break.

• *Extent* questions. Mr. Blackwell uses *extent* questions to collect further relevant information about the problem. Some of these questions do not apply to this case. For example, the *is* question that asks, How many deviations are on each object?— and its corresponding *is not* question—do not make sense in this situation. The next question asks about the trend of the problem: Is it getting worse, better, or staying the same?

Narrow Possible Causes

We generally have little difficulty surmising what might cause a problem. We find it more difficult to evaluate these theories rationally and rigorously, using factual information. This evaluation step helps us use the facts we gathered in the previous step to eliminate causes that don't stack up against the evidence.

Narrowing possible causes occurs in two parts. First, we answer the question, What could have caused the problem? We want to formulate specific hypotheses about what could have caused the problem and then *list* those hypotheses.

Type of Question	Is Questions	Is Not Questions
What	What specific object (or objects) has the deviation?	What similar object (or objects) could reasonably have the deviation, but does not?
	What is the specific deviation?	What other deviations could reasonably be observed, but are not?
Where	Where is the object when the deviation is observed (geographically)?	Where else could the object be located when the deviation is observed, but is not?
	Where is the deviation on the object?	Where else could the deviation be located on the object, but is not?
When	When was the deviation observed first (in clock and calendar time)?	When else could the deviation have been observed first, but was not?
	When since that time has the deviation been observed? Any pattern?	When since that time could the deviation have been observed, but was not?
	When, in the object's history or life cycle, was the deviation observed first?	When else, in the object's history or life cycle, could the deviation have been observed first, but was not?
Extent	How many objects have the deviation?	How many objects could have the deviation, but do not?
	What is the size of a single deviation?	What other size could the deviation be, but is not?
	How many deviations are on each object?	How many deviations could there be on each object, but are not?
	What is the trend?	What could be the trend, but is not?

FIGURE 5.2
Is and Is Not Questions

Second, we *test* the possible causes by comparing them to our *is/is not* information and asking, If _____ is the cause, how does it explain both the *is* and *is not* information? When we test our causes, three possible outcomes emerge:

• The cause explains all the *is/is not* information.

• The cause explains certain *is/is not* facts only if certain elements are true (e.g., if we make certain assumptions).

75

	FIGURE 5.3	
	***Is* and *Is Not* Questions Applied to the Math Lab Example**	

Type of Question	*Is* Questions and Information	*Is Not* Questions and Information
What	What specific object (or objects) has the deviation? *Math lab students in 7th and 8th grades.*	What similar object (or objects) could reasonably have the deviation, but does not? *Math lab students in 5th and 6th grades.*
	What is the specific deviation? *Not progressing—minimal improvement on entering scores.*	What other deviations could reasonably be observed, but are not? *High absenteeism and disruptive behavior.*
Where	Where is the object when the deviation is observed (geographically)? *Math lab.*	Where else could the object be located when the deviation is observed, but is not? *In class.*
	Where is the deviation on the object? *N/A.*	Where else could the deviation be located on the object, but is not? *N/A.*
When	When was the deviation observed first (in clock and calendar time)? *January 5, 2000 (after winter break).*	When else could the deviation have been observed first, but was not? *Before January 5, 2000.*
	When since that time has the deviation been observed? Any pattern? *Continuous.*	When since that time could the deviation have been observed, but was not? *Sporadic or a specific pattern.*
	When, in the object's history or life cycle, was the deviation observed first? *After winter break.*	When else, in the object's history or life cycle, could the deviation have been observed first, but was not? *Before winter break.*
Extent	How many objects have the deviation? *85% of 7th grade; 79% of 8th grade.*	How many objects could have the deviation, but do not? *More or less.*
	What is the size of a single deviation? *Have not progressed one grade level.*	What other size could the deviation be, but is not? *More or less than one grade level.*
	How many deviations are on each object? *N/A.*	How many deviations could there be on each object, but are not? *N/A.*
	What is the trend? *Getting worse.*	What could be the trend, but is not? *Getting better or staying the same.*

• The cause does not explain certain *is/is not* facts.

When narrowing possible causes, we try to eliminate causes. If a possibility does not make sense, let's not consider it further. When we eliminate unviable possibilities, we save a lot of time and effort later. Notice that the *is not* information forces us to consider a cause or allows us to rule it out. If we did not have the *is not* information—if we had only to consider the *is* information—we could explain just about any cause. When we force a cause to explain both the *is* and the *is not* information, we see which causes make more sense.

Applying the Process:
Math Lab Example

Mr. Blackwell talks with the math lab team and others to collect ideas about what could cause the lack of progress. Here are some possible causes:

- The math lab concept is ineffective.
- Students spend too little time in the lab.
- Students have spring fever.
- New software is ineffective for 7th and 8th grade students.

Figure 5.4 (p. 78) shows how Mr. Blackwell tests these possible causes against the *is* and *is not* facts. He immediately eliminates the possible cause, Math lab concept is ineffective. That cause doesn't explain why it was effective, even for 7th and 8th grade students, before January and why it still is effective for 5th and 6th grade students. He also eliminates spring fever as a cause. The problem was first noticed in January. Furthermore, the cause doesn't seem to explain why only 7th and 8th grade

students are affected. Mr. Blackwell is left with two possible causes as he moves on to the next step.

Determine the True Cause

Before we make significant changes, we want to be sure we identify the true cause. After we evaluate our possible causes, we identify the cause that seems to make the most sense. This is our most likely cause. Generally, this is the possible cause with the fewest or least outrageous assumptions attached (those listed in Column 2 of Figure 5.4 on p. 78).

After we have identified the most likely cause, we ask, What can we do to determine if our most likely cause is indeed our true cause? Often, all we need to do is simply check to see if the assumptions we have made (those listed in Column 2 of Figure 5.4) while testing are true. At other times, we might observe the situation to determine if we can verify the true cause. We can verify the true cause by following these steps:

• Gathering additional facts to check assumptions made while testing. Gathering additional information *before* we make changes is generally more cost effective and less disruptive. We can often use these facts to prove or disprove the assumptions made while testing possible causes.

• Making a change and checking to see if the problem goes away.

Applying the Process:
Math Lab Example

Based on the assumptions associated with the two remaining causes, Mr. Blackwell isn't sure which

> ### FIGURE 5.4
> ### Narrowing Possible Causes in the Math Lab Example
>
> | Possible Cause | Possible cause could explain the deviation if the following assumptions are true: | Possible cause does not explain the deviation because . . . |
> |---|---|---|
> | The math lab concept is ineffective. | | Students in 7th and 8th grades were making good progress before January.

Students in 5th and 6th grades are still making good progress. |
> | Students spend too little time in the lab. | Students in 7th and 8th grades spent more time before January.

Students in 5th and 6th grades now spend more time than students in 7th and 8th grades. | |
> | Students have spring fever. | | Problem started in January.

Only 7th and 8th grade students are affected. |
> | New software is ineffective for 7th and 8th grade students. | Software was installed around the time of winter break.

Only 7th and 8th grade students are using the new software. | |

cause is most likely; he decides to investigate both. In other instances, one cause jumps out and seems to make more sense: Maybe it makes fewer assumptions or the assumptions are less outrageous. Mr. Blackwell investigates further to gather additional facts for checking the assumptions.

He takes the possible cause, New software is ineffective for 7th and 8th grade students, and checks the assumptions made in Column 2 of Figure 5.4. He finds that the new software was installed in March, two months after the problem first appeared. He also learns that the software is used

by all grade levels. Mr. Blackwell eliminates this cause.

He checks into the possible cause, Students spend too little time in the lab. He determines that the 7th and 8th grade students' lab time has been cut significantly since December. They now spend only 15 minutes in the lab; they used to spend 30 minutes, the amount of time the 5th and 6th grade students currently spend. The amount of time certainly seems to be insufficient. He further validates this cause by observing students in the lab: He finds that by the time the students are settled in front of the computers, log on, decide what they are going to do, and read instructions, they spend less than 7 minutes doing anything related to math.

Mr. Blackwell determines that the true cause of the problem is the shortened time, which has reduced the effectiveness of the lab for 7th and 8th grade students. Apparently, 15 minutes is not enough time for the students to make progress. He shares these findings with Ms. Testa. She is surprised, because she was one of the main proponents of reducing the time. She believed that any amount of time was better than no time, and the reduced lab time would give greater access to more 7th and 8th grade students. She is stunned by the small amount of time they actually engage in math activities. After seeing the results, she concludes that 15 minutes of lab time is too short a time to make a difference.

Problem Analysis Refinements

Most of the time, the basic steps of problem analysis are all we need to understand a problem well enough to find the true cause. Sometimes, however, a problem is so complex or baffling that we need help to identify possible causes.

Recall one of our original conditions for a problem—that it involves a change or a deviation from what should happen and what actually happens. For a while, progress in the math lab might have been fine. But then, performance dropped off. In short, a change occurred.

The problem analysis refinements help us search for *relevant* change—that is, the change or changes that cause the actual performance to deviate from the desired performance. Because situations change constantly, looking at all changes that took place could be overwhelming. When

we focus on changes directly related to the problem, we find important clues about what causes the problem.

Figure 5.5 (p. 80) shows the flow of basic problem analysis steps and where the problem analysis refinements fit in. Usually, if we have already used the basic problem analysis steps and identified and verified the true cause, we have little need to go back and use distinctions and changes. Distinctions and changes are useful after we identify *is* and *is not* data to generate possible causes, or if we have tried the basic steps and haven't been able to find the true cause.

Identifying Distinctions and Changes

Imagine two identical houseplants; one is thriving and the other is dying. Instinctively, we look at what is different about the dying plant (e.g., its location and watering schedule). After all, there has to be a reason that one plant is dying. Something has to be different about the dying plant to contribute to its demise. Further investigation reveals that the dying houseplant is close to a heating vent. Maybe it has happily sat next to the heating vent for six months. If the weather has recently gotten cold enough to turn on the heat, however, something has changed. Therefore, the fact that the plant is next to the heating vent, which was recently activated, may be the cause of the plant's poor health.

In problem solving, after we gather the *is* and *is not* information, we might find ourselves wondering, What is different or unique about the *is* when compared to the *is not*? When we ask this question, we are looking for distinctions—those qualities or characteristics that make the *is* different from the *is not*. Typically, they jump out at us. We can look at each set of

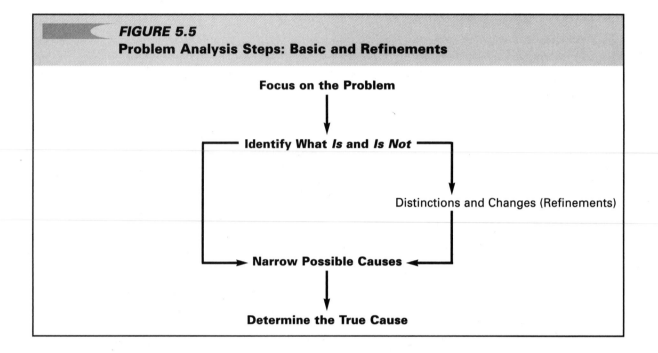

FIGURE 5.5
Problem Analysis Steps: Basic and Refinements

Focus on the Problem

Identify What *Is* and *Is Not*

Distinctions and Changes (Refinements)

Narrow Possible Causes

Determine the True Cause

is/is not facts and look for distinctions. We might find only one or two.

After we have identified distinctions, we examine each distinction and ask, What has changed in, on, around, or about this distinction? We look only for changes in our distinctions to ensure we identify changes directly relevant to the problem. It is helpful to date the changes so we can see how they correlate with the appearance of the problem. Not every distinction will have a change associated with it.

Applying the Process: Math Lab Example

If you have already found the true cause, without using distinctions and changes (as Mr. Blackwell did), there would usually be no need for them. But to show how they could apply, we'll re-

visit the math lab example. Let's assume Mr. Blackwell has just finished gathering *is* and *is not* information and decided to use distinctions and changes.

Mr. Blackwell reviews the *is* and *is not* information he has gathered (shown in Figure 5.3). He realizes he's learned some interesting facts that don't necessarily answer the *is* and *is not* questions. He's learned that the 7th and 8th grade math lab students spend less time in the lab than do the other students They spend only 15 minutes in the lab, while the 5th and 6th grade students spend 30 minutes. Another fact he discovered was that many more 7th and 8th grade students use the lab than 5th and 6th grade students (359 seventh and eighth grade students compared to 110 fifth and sixth grade students. These are both distinctions in the *what* category (a common source of distinctions) and are the only distinctions he finds.

Mr. Blackwell questions the math lab team and learns that the lab time for 7th and 8th grade students was reduced from 30 minutes to 15 minutes shortly before the holiday break in December. This change was made to ensure that the lab was available to all 7th and 8th grade students who wanted access. Figure 5.6 (p. 82) shows how *is* and *is not* information from Figure 5.3 can be used to create a completed specification containing distinctions and changes.

Using Distinctions and Changes to Develop Possible Causes

We use distinctions and changes to generate possible causes. If we can identify some distinctions and changes, we can use them to gain ideas about what might have caused the problem. Here are questions we ask to identify possible causes: How could this change have caused the problem? How could this change plus a distinction have caused the problem? How could this change plus another change have caused the problem?

After we identify possible causes, the rest of the process is identical to the steps in problem analysis explained earlier: We narrow the possible causes by testing them against the *is/is not* data and determine the true cause by verifying whether our most likely cause is indeed the true cause.

Applying the Process:
Math Lab Example

When Mr. Blackwell sees the *distinction* of less time coupled with the *change* in timing— when the lab time was reduced—he theorizes that 15 minutes is insufficient time for the students to use the lab productively. He tests this cause against the *is* and *is not* facts in Figure 5.3. For ex-

ample, if it's true that 15 minutes is insufficient time to use the lab productively, does it explain both the *is* and *is not* facts? He also tests the other causes that people have mentioned (see Narrow Possible Causes section). His hypothesis becomes his most likely cause, which he then verifies (see Determine the True Cause section). He shares these results with Ms. Testa.

Applying Problem Analysis in Schools

We have examined the steps of problem analysis and looked at how it might apply in a school situation. In this section, we see examples of how administrators and teachers have put the ideas to use.

Examples of Administrative Use

Gathering data for more effective problem solving. The curriculum coordinator at a Louisiana school was disappointed when many of her 4th grade students failed the math portion of the Louisiana Educational Assessment Program (LEAP) test, the high-stakes test students must pass to be promoted to the 5th grade. Of all 4th grade students, 49 percent made "unsatisfactory" scores on the test. This was the first year the test had been given at her school, which is a semirural school of 760 students. Twenty percent of the students receive some special education services, and 90 percent qualify for free or reduced lunches. The 4th grade population mirrors that of the school. There are four 4th grade teachers. Each 4th grade class is self-contained, but planning is done by grade level. Teachers are free to teach skills as they see fit, using their own teaching styles and techniques.

> **FIGURE 5.6**
> **Distinctions and Changes in the Math Lab Example**

Type of Question	*Is* Information	*Is Not* Information	Distinctions	Changes
What	Math lab students in 7th and 8th grades. Not progressing—minimal improvement on entering scores.	Math lab students in 5th and 6th grades. High absenteeism and disruptive behavior.	More students in math lab. Less time in math lab.	No known change. Time reduced in December 1999.
Where	Math lab. N/A.	In class. N/A.		
When	January 5, 2000 (after winter break). Continuous. After winter break.	Before January 5, 2000. Sporadic or a specific pattern. Before winter break.		
Extent	85% of 7th grade; 79% of 8th grade. Have not progressed one grade level. N/A. Getting worse.	More or less. More or less. N/A. Getting better or staying the same.		

The curriculum coordinator saw the unsatisfactory test scores as an opportunity to apply problem analysis. She began to collect information by classroom, asking, "Which specific students failed the LEAP test?" She decided to focus first on the regular student population. She found that 35 percent of Teacher A's regular students scored "unsatisfactory," 25 percent of Teacher B's, 24 percent of Teacher C's, and 67 percent of Teacher D's. She began to wonder, Why do Teacher D's 4th grade students have such a high failure rate on LEAP math? Here's her problem statement: Teacher D's 4th grade students have a high failure rate on the math portion of the LEAP test. She gathered even more data. Figure 5.7 (p. 84) shows the *is* and *is not* information, distinctions, and changes she identified—the problem specification.

The curriculum coordinator then tested several possible causes that she and others had identified. Figure 5.8 (p. 85) shows the results. The most probable cause was that Teacher D was not skilled in the new teaching techniques for math. To determine if that was indeed the cause, the curriculum coordinator conducted classroom observations and consultations with Teacher D. These actions confirmed that this teacher, although strong in other areas, was not strong in math teaching techniques.

The thorough job the curriculum coordinator did in collecting information and using it productively helped turn a difficult situation into one that could be dealt with constructively. It would have been easy for Teacher D to feel singled out and threatened. But the data spoke for themselves. They weren't someone's interpretation of her teaching performance or assessment; they were facts. The curriculum coordinator assured Teacher D that her efforts were valued; the school just wanted to help her become as effective as possible. The teacher was scheduled for special training over the summer to help her develop her math teaching skills. Next year, her math classes and student results will be tracked to ensure that progress is made.

Using distinctions and changes to identify the most significant contributing factors. The assistant principal of a middle school in Terrebonne Parish (Louisiana) noticed an unusually high increase in the number of disciplinary referrals from the library. He went through the files and talked with the librarian and others to collect relevant *is* and *is not* data. In-

trigued that disciplinary referrals had not increased from anywhere else, he looked at what made the library distinct or unique. Figure 5.9 (p. 86) shows the information he collected in his problem specification.

The assistant principal showed the librarian the information and asked for her thoughts and ideas. The librarian proposed new strategies. She worked with each class to develop, post, and discuss expectations for conduct in the library, and she began to use lesson plans. The librarian and students felt ownership in the solutions because they had been involved in the process. After these solutions were implemented, disciplinary referrals from the library dropped by almost 50 percent.

Opening eyes through *is/is not* questioning. In Orange County, Florida, a rash of seven pedestrian accidents involving school-age children occurred during September and October 1999. Because all seven accidents happened before sunrise, many in the community made the logical assumption that changing the school start time to later in the morning, when it would be light, would prevent further accidents. The communitywide task force, formed to study the problem, discovered that other factors were at work in addition to lighting conditions. They made this discovery by asking the critical questions of problem analysis.

Pressure increased to change the school start time, but task force members believed it was important to have the facts. They wanted to get the most accurate information possible. They spent some time rewording the *is* and *is not* questions to ensure that people unfamiliar with problem analysis could easily provide the information they needed. Figure 5.10 (p. 87) shows the reworded questions.

FIGURE 5.7

Problem Specification in the LEAP Scores Example

Type of Question	*Is* Information	*Is Not* Information	Distinctions	Changes
What	Teacher D's students.	Teacher A, B, or C's students.	Teacher D, who is • Newer to school (two years versus average of six years). • Not trained in new math teaching techniques.	
	Failed math portions of LEAP test; worse on number relations, data analysis, geometry, and patterns.	As bad on algebra and measurement, other LEAP subjects, and teacher-made math tests.		
Where	Teacher D's classroom. N/A.	Other classrooms. N/A.		
When	May 1999. N/A (single event). End of school year; math portion given last.	Before May 1999. N/A. Earlier in school year; earlier in testing.		
Extent	17 of 25. Scored below 40th percentile; ranged from 28 to 39. Four of six strands. Need more data.	More or less than 17. Lower than 28 to 39. More or less than four strands. Need more data.		

By asking *is* and *is not* questions, several important assumptions were revised. The problem statement went through several revisions as the problem became clearer. The task force soon realized that the problem was pedestrian safety, a much broader and more complex problem than

the safety of children on their way to school. Here are some of the significant facts these critical questions revealed:

• During the 11-month period for which data were analyzed, 305 pedestrian accidents

FIGURE 5.8
Narrowing Possible Causes in the LEAP Scores Example

Possible Cause	Test by Asking, Does This Possible Cause Make Sense?
This school's students are just weak in math.	No. Only Teacher D's students did so much worse than students in other classes.
Teacher D is an ineffective teacher.	No. Her students scored poorly only in math.
Teacher D is not skilled in new teaching techniques for math.	Maybe. Test against *is/is not* information cannot be ruled out.
The LEAP test is a new test with a different format.	No. The other three classes scored significantly better.
More disadvantaged students are in Teacher D's class.	No. Demographic mix is evenly distributed among classes.

occurred. Adult pedestrians were involved in 77 percent of these accidents; school-age children were involved in 23 percent.

• Safety measures were present at 78 percent of the accident sites.

• In 41 percent of the accidents, unsafe or illegal actions on the part of the driver were involved.

• Of these accidents, 60 percent occurred in daylight, a surprising fact, because most of the community believed darkness was a major factor. For school-age children, only 35 percent of the accidents occurred in limited lighting conditions.

• For adult pedestrians, 63 percent of the accidents involved unsafe or illegal actions by the pedestrian.

• For school-age pedestrians, 87 percent of the accidents involved unsafe or illegal actions by the pedestrian.

The task force developed charts that showed the time of each accident and overlaid a graph of sunrise times on the charts. These actions allowed the task force to see the contribution of limited lighting to the number of accidents. Possible causes (lighting conditions, driver actions, pedestrian actions, and availability of safety measures) were tested against the data. A sense began to emerge that all the factors contributed to some degree, but not in the proportions people assumed before the data were analyzed.

Simply changing school start times would potentially prevent only some of the future accidents. Gathering facts helped the community understand that this problem was complex and deserved a multifaceted solution. The school district worked with the public works department and others to develop solutions that included changing school start times, educating children about pedestrian safety, and ensuring availability

FIGURE 5.9
Problem Specification in the Disciplinary Referrals Example

Type of Question	*Is* Information	*Is Not* Information	Distinctions	Changes
What	Students numbered 1–58 on a list. Disruptive behavior: talking, getting out of seat, fighting, and disobeying.	Other students. Cutting class and being tardy.		
Where	In library. N/A.	As bad in other areas: gym, classrooms, lunchroom, band, and computer lab. N/A.	No posted rules, no grades given on report card (either academic or conduct), no lesson plans used, and no tests given.	No known change.
When	August 1999. Continuous. Usually started after first 10 minutes of class and took place throughout rest of class.	Before August 1999. Erratic or periodic. In first 10 minutes of class.	New librarian (new to that school; she had six years' experience at another school).	Hired new librarian in summer of 1999.
Extent	About 10% of students. Bad enough to disrupt class. One to six referrals apiece. Number of referrals per week remaining about the same.	More or less than 10%. Less than that. More or less than one to six referrals apiece. Getting better or worse.		

of safety measures (e.g., crosswalks, sidewalks, and traffic signals). The data showed clearly that a more effective and comprehensive solution was needed for this serious problem.

Using facts to diffuse emotion. The director of exceptional student education (ESE) in an urban school district received a call from a representative in the local juvenile justice system. The

FIGURE 5.10
Is and *Is Not* Questions in the Pedestrian Safety Example

Type of Question	*Is* Questions	*Is Not* Questions
What	Who are the victims in accidents involving pedestrians?	Who might we expect as victims but aren't?
	What is the nature of an accident?	What might we expect the nature of an accident to be, but don't see?
Where	Where exactly are these accidents occurring?	Where might we expect them to occur?
When	When did these accidents first occur?	When might we have expected them to start occurring?
	When during the day do they occur?	When might we expect them to occur?
Extent	How many accidents have there been?	How many might we have expected?
	What is the extent of damage?	What might the extent have been, but wasn't?
	What is the trend?	What might the trend have been, but wasn't?

caller wanted to know why so many children under age 12 were being arrested at the special schools for severely emotionally disturbed students. The director was interested in learning more, so she pulled together a team that included administrators, paraprofessionals, behavior specialists, and teachers. Emotions ran high because children being arrested created a lot of attention within the community and with the media. The people involved felt unfairly criticized and misunderstood. Most of them believed that others, such as neglectful parents, overzealous law enforcement officials, or story-hungry media, were to blame.

Initially, the problem appeared to be that many children were being arrested. As team members prepared to apply problem analysis, however, they realized they already knew *why* the students were being arrested: The students had exhibited extremely violent behavior that included danger to or direct attacks on school employees. Focus of the discussion quickly turned from the arrests to the behavior. This change of focus allowed group members to concentrate on the students and the reasons these incidents were escalating, rather than on the negative attention and criticism they received from other adults.

The *is/is not* questions allowed them to direct their investigation toward behavior and why it occurred, first by understanding more about the behavior. What specific behavior was involved? When did it occur? Was there a pattern? Did the behavior tend to occur in certain places? When the team focused on facts, the individuals felt less threatened and defensive. That focus helped move the discussion from the question, Why are so many children being arrested? to, Let's take a look at what exactly is happening. This focus on facts helped depersonalize the situation.

Figure 5.11 shows the team's initial pass at completing the *is/is not* problem specification. Notice the areas where they identify a need for more data (indicated by TBD—to be determined). They then identified the specific questions they needed to ask to get the missing data (see italicized questions in Figure 5.11). The specification clearly shows exactly what pieces of data they needed to collect (e.g., when during the week most arrests occur and when during the week they are least likely to occur). This work helped focus their data collection efforts. Knowing they would get the facts and have some answers helped turn what might have been a volatile meeting full of finger-pointing into one where people could move forward cooperatively.

Other administrative examples. Examples of other situations in which problem analysis has been useful include the following:

• A high school assistant principal conducted a problem analysis on why an unusually high number of students scored low on the graduation exit exam. People initially theorized that the reason was that the math section was completed on the last day of three days of testing, or that this was the first year the special education

students were required to take the test. When the assistant principal gathered and analyzed data, however, she found that most low-scoring high school students (73 percent) were from the same junior high school, and the problem existed before the special education students took the test this year. She was able quickly to lay to rest two popular theories.

• An elementary school principal conducted a problem analysis on why parental attendance was always low at open houses. School officials first thought low attendance represented low parental interest and support. But when they collected data from parents and others, they found that transportation was a major issue; parents could not easily get to school from outlying rural locations. After the school district ran school buses along certain routes, parental attendance increased greatly.

• A team used problem analysis to investigate the increased number of students who attended schools outside their attendance zone. To gather better data on the problem, team members reworded the *is/is not* questions to use in community focus groups.

• A guidance counselor used problem analysis to examine the sudden onset of a student's behavioral problems. The student had been a model student. After the counselor collected data, a distinct pattern of when the outbursts occurred emerged. After talking with the student and his divorced parents, the counselor saw that the incidents were worse after the student spent weekends with his father.

Examples of Classroom Use

Understanding a situation and its effect. A middle school class in Phillipsburg, New Jersey, is reading *Maudie and Me and the Dirty Book* (Miles, 1980). The book is about two 6th grade

FIGURE 5.11
Problem Specification in the Student Arrests Example

Type of Question	*Is* Information	*Is Not* Information
What	ESE students 12 years old and under with classification of exceptionalities a, b, d, and f.	ESE students with classification of exceptionalities c, e, g, and h.
	Increasing arrests.	Increasing suspensions and expulsions; declining attendance.
Where	Schools A and B: centers for severely emotionally disturbed students.	Other center schools: those for students with other exceptionalities.
	Classrooms, bus ramp area, PE fields, transition areas (halls), and lunchroom.	Restrooms, front offices, nurse's office, crisis assembly points, media center, and tech lab; low class-size situations.
When	1999–2000 SY (school year).	Prior to 1999–2000 SY.
	August 1999 through December 1999.	As bad January to March 2000.
	Worst immediately before and after holidays.	Longer periods before and after holidays.
	When during the week did most arrests occur?	*When during the week were arrests least likely to occur?*
	What time of day did most arrests occur?	*What time of day were arrests least likely to occur?*
Extent	15% of population (12 years old and under).	85% of population (12 years old and under).
	What was average number of arrests during a specified time frame?	*What was average number of days with no arrests?*
	Number involved in multiple arrests.	N/A.

Note: ESE = exceptional student education.

girls, Kate and Maudie, who read a book to 1st grade students. The 1st grade parents get upset.

The class teachers decide to use problem analysis to help their students understand why the parents got upset. The teachers first introduce the concept of what a problem is: the difference between what should happen (what we'd like to have happen) and what actually happens.

The teachers ask the students for examples of problems they've experienced.

Next, they ask the students, Who in the novel is having the problem? What is the problem they are having? The class focuses on the following problem statement: Maudie and Kate read a dirty book.

The students form small groups. The teachers then pose a modified version of the *is/is not* questions, tailored for the scenario. Students learn to see problems as a difference in what should happen and what actually happens and to gather key information in four areas (what, where, when, and to what extent) so they can fully understand a situation and its effect. They brainstorm possible causes and compare them to the *is* and *is not* information to see which causes make the most sense.

Problems and perspective. To help students realize that problems may be different, depending on the students' perspectives, two middle school language arts teachers have students define and examine a problem from the point of view of three different characters. The class is reading *Nothing but the Truth* (Avi, 1991). Each group of students is assigned a different character, and group members define the problem as that character sees it. Then they gather *is* and *is not* information based on actual events, facts, and quotes in the book. This activity encourages students to be specific, to separate fact from conjecture, and to see that different people can view the same events from different angles—what constitutes a problem from one person's perspective means something different to another.

Finding the true cause is the only way we can ensure that a problem will not arise again.

Whether we are administrators who deal with a sudden drop in student enrollment or students who examine the factors that led to the Holocaust, we need to understand the causes in order to learn. If an airplane crashes, understanding what caused the crash will not bring back the lives lost. The Federal Aviation Administration probes to find the cause for the crash so that what they learn may prevent future loss of life.

Problem analysis helps us solve problems by encouraging us to first focus on facts instead of conjecture. When things go wrong, people theorize about what happened and why. As they explain and defend their theories, they become invested in being right. To justify their rationale, they use data that support their theory (and ignore data that refute it). Others may propose alternative theories. Soon, problem solving is about proving we are right, not determining what went wrong. The problem becomes unnecessarily personalized. Problem analysis allows us to minimize the chances of that happening by encouraging us to gather facts before we focus on theories.

Problem analysis is not possible without factual information or data. Typically, a wealth of information is available. Often, though, we are unaware of what information is available, where it is, or how to use it. Problem analysis helps us define specific data we need. Once we know what data we need, we can more easily determine who may have them and how to get them. Sometimes simple observation can go a long way. Think about the math lab example: By watching what the 7th and 8th grade students were actually doing during their 15 minutes in the lab, Mr. Blackwell determined how little time students were involved in math activities.

Just as common as the emotional investment that affects problem solving is the drive to take action, regardless of how effective it may be. Sometimes, taking swift and decisive action— doing anything—is prized more highly than taking the time necessary to ensure the action will eliminate the problem. Problem analysis helps ensure that the changes we make to fix a problem are really changes that will *eliminate* the problem.

Good problem solving also means involving others effectively. Typically, no single person has all the information or all the answers. We need other people to help solve problems, and problem analysis provides a framework for involving others in the problem-solving process. When we need the *information* that others have, we ask specific questions to help determine whom we need to involve or ask. We also need others for the *ideas* they may have about what might have caused the problem. Whether we are gathering data or collecting theories, other people are a critical part of the process. Our ability to ask good questions is fundamental to successfully involving others.

Problem analysis helps us avoid unnecessary action, or action that may actually create more problems than it solves. It forces us to slow down and learn about the problem before we jump to some kind of solution. Problem analysis helps us appreciate the role of facts in problem solving and the benefits of finding the true cause.

Situation Appraisal:
What's Going On?
Sorting Out Complexity

Problems often arise when we are least prepared to handle them. They are sometimes not as they first appear. We might think we understand what we're dealing with, but when we pull away the layers, we find something completely different. To make a situation more complicated, others may disagree with how we want to approach the problem. Solving problems can be like ordering an unfamiliar dish in a foreign land: We don't know what it is we were just served, what's in it, or how to eat it.

Situation appraisal is a tool to help us clarify and manage the problems that face us. It helps us better understand a situation or issue and prepare to address it. Think about the complexity and the many layers of the issues with which you are faced: raising student achievement, finding the best ways to assess student progress, trying to find sources of new funds, and combating school violence. We need a tool to help us assess situations such as these because complex issues are typically a tangle of divergent elements, opinions, priorities, possibilities, and needs.

Generalities: Not a Good Way to Deal with Complexity

The most common pitfall for people who deal with complex situations and issues is that they fail to see all the pieces of the puzzle with equal clarity. We are tempted to make a snap judgment about a situation or to believe we understand it. We often lump things together with a label we believe sums up the whole problem—the morale problem or the communications issue. But we can rarely sum up or grasp complicated issues so easily. When we do not adequately see and deal with the specific elements of multifaceted and difficult issues, we can face significant consequences. Here are some of them:

• *Overlooking critical elements.* If we are not able or willing to examine each critical piece of an issue, the overlooked piece may prove to be the most consequential. Only when we see the entire picture can we set priorities and assess the importance of each part.

• *Focusing on minutiae.* When faced with generalities or massive issues, people will sometimes attack relatively unimportant elements. Because the real and persistent issues may be too unclear for us to adequately address, the minutia may get the attention. Such a response is the equivalent of rearranging the deck chairs on the *Titanic*. The deck chairs may need rearranging, but in light of the current situation, what difference does it make? We see this type of action often: Well-intentioned and earnest people want to do something. But how much more powerful could these same people be if they channeled those tendencies toward not just doing *some*thing, but doing the *right* thing?

• *Procrastinating.* Another possible consequence of not looking at the specific elements of an issue—of being too general—is that the situation at hand can seem so overwhelming and massive that no one does anything. After all, exactly how *do* you deal with the issue of the breakdown of the family or student achievement? Other emergencies and issues always arise that require our attention. Unless we break each of these massive, yet critically important, issues into manageable components we can act upon,

we may always be distracted by the day-to-day demands that divert our attention.

• *Not understanding others.* Complex issues often involve multiple and divergent perspectives and opinions. The only way to understand the issue is to pull these multiple strands apart and examine them. Volume and intensity often rise in proportion to the complexity of an issue. In such situations, we need to show people we have heard their arguments and ideas. When people know they have been heard, they are better prepared to listen.

• *Not resolving conflict.* People tend to shy away from conflict or attempt to keep it under control by not giving it a chance to arise. One way to avoid conflict is to deal in generalities. If we don't provide an opportunity for people to deal with specifics, so the thinking goes, we minimize the chance that conflict will result. The problem is, we also minimize the chance that the conflict will get resolved. And the longer people's emotions simmer without an outlet, the greater the force of the eventual eruption. When complex issues generate conflict, we must bring this conflict to the surface and address it.

Situation appraisal is a process that pulls apart the strands that comprise the issues we face so we can determine how to deal with each individual strand. It is a tool to help us identify, understand, and set issues in order of priority, as well as to identify possible next steps to deal with them. As you read this chapter, consider the following ways situation appraisal helps us:

• Examining an issue in greater depth.
• Bringing to the surface opinions or feelings about an emotional issue.
• Understanding better what is on people's minds.

• Getting started on an assignment or project.

• Assessing implementation of a prior or ongoing project or initiative.

• Addressing complex situations.

Remember the old saying, "How do you eat an elephant? One bite at a time." Situation appraisal helps us carve the issues into bite-sized, manageable pieces. Issues seldom arrive that way.

A Scenario for Situation Appraisal

It is late January in the Willow River School District. The superintendent has assembled a high-profile task force to deal with the issue of school violence. Several recent incidents of school violence around the country have heightened public awareness and concern over this issue. The most recent tragedy left several students dead. Fortunately, the district has never had a serious incident of school violence. But people realize they can no longer maintain the attitude that it won't happen in their district. Student and parent fears are growing. Parents have threatened to pull their children out of school all together. The community, like many throughout the United States, has been severely shaken and tested.

The task force has spent a couple of weeks holding focus groups and talking with students, parents, teachers, staff, and other community members. Although everyone is united in their concern about school violence, huge variations exist in how people think the problem should be addressed. Some parents favor metal detectors at all schools; others believe metal detectors would send a distorted message to students and outsiders. The district has been considering a

school uniform policy, and there is dissension about that. Students don't want their rights limited, and parents are divided on the issue. The only factor that unites everyone is their desire to prevent violence in a district school.

The task force knows it is critical for the district to approach this issue comprehensively, responsively, and in a timely manner. As with many high-threat, high-visibility issues, the situation must be handled effectively; otherwise, the results may mirror the ones listed here:

• Alienation of stakeholders who believe their concerns are not adequately aired or heard.

• Lack of support for proposed solutions.

• Various factions not listening to others or denigrating others and their issues.

• Diminished confidence in school and district leadership.

• Increased tension among stakeholder groups.

• Chaos.

• Lack of effective action against the issue at hand.

• Increased negative publicity about the district and its leadership.

The Steps in Situation Appraisal

We use the acronym SCAN to describe the steps of situation appraisal. The process involves four primary steps (shown earlier in Figure 1.4):

• **S**ee the issues.
• **C**larify the issues.
• **A**ssess priorities.
• **N**ame next steps.

Let's look more closely at these steps and how they apply to the scenario about school violence.

See the Issues

To help us understand what we are dealing with, we identify the issues we face in a particular situation by asking key questions such as, What seems to be important about this situation? What concerns need to be examined or addressed? Sometimes issues are handed to us, and what we need to work on is clear. A complicated situation, however, may spawn a multitude of issues. Important stakeholders may not verbalize their concerns. The unrecognized issue cannot be addressed, yet it may be the one that is the most significant in the long run.

When we deal with an emotionally volatile situation, asking angry stakeholders for their opinions can be scary. Some may view the request as adding fuel to the fire, but in reality, the opposite is true. When people feel ignored or misunderstood, their emotions rise. Remember, we don't eliminate conflict by pretending it doesn't exist. We may not be comfortable handling conflict, but it doesn't go away because we don't want to experience it. Rather, conflict that is ignored or pushed underground festers and spreads. Lack of support for new initiatives, undermining others' efforts, and increasing polarization of stakeholder groups are examples of fallout from unresolved conflicts. When we get the issues on the table, at least we know what we're dealing with. When we know what we're dealing with, we can take reasonable and appropriate action.

Applying the Process:
School Violence Example

The task force decides to use situation appraisal to deal with this important issue. Everyone takes out their notes from focus groups and other discussions. One member of the group records the issues as group members share what they have found. Members have identified important and varied issues relating to school violence. In their final list, the task force identified 18 issues, including these:

- Safety precautions.
- School uniforms.
- Identification of staff, students, and visitors.
- Upcoming prom.
- Recent threats.

These issues are listed in Column 1 of Figure 6.1 (p. 96). For this discussion, we follow only these issues through the rest of the situation appraisal process. Obviously, the task force needed to address all 18 issues.

Clarify the Issues

Sometimes when issues arise, they are clearly stated and easily understood (e.g., choose a faculty advisor for the dance or find missing tests). At other times, the issues are not clear (e.g., school spirit). We might believe we know what an issue means, but we might not know what another person means when they state an issue. For example, to a principal, the issue of diversity might mean how to make all ethnic groups within a school feel equally welcome. A teacher might interpret diversity as a lack of sensitivity to a given minority group. A parent might be concerned about the apparent lack of diversity among a school's population. All these interpretations are equally valid, yet they differ. In addition, complex issues are usually made up of several subissues. We need to be sure we understand what an issue means and what its components are before we can determine how to most effectively deal with it.

FIGURE 6.1			
Situation Appraisal in the School Violence Example			

See the Issues	Clarify the Issues	Assess Priorities	Name Next Steps
Safety precautions	What precautions are in place to screen for guns? How do we identify at-risk students? What can we learn from other districts' experiences? Are students and staff given emergency drills?	*	*What:* Investigate safety vulnerabilities and identify possible solutions. *Who:* Safety task force. *By when:* March 1.
School uniforms	Are we going to have school uniforms? Are we going to limit individuals' freedom of expression?		
Identification of staff, students, and visitors	How do we know who should and shouldn't be on school grounds? What is current district policy? Do we need a system of identification?	*	*What:* Develop consistent districtwide identification policy. Select best identification system. *Who:* Assistant superintendent and principals. *By when:* April 30.
Upcoming prom	What do we know about tensions increasing between student cliques? What do we know about rumors of possible disturbance at the prom?		*What:* Work with prom committee and security to identify possible problems and ways to address them. *Who:* Faculty advisor. *By when:* March 1.
Recent threats	Where are they coming from? What's current policy? Do we need severe consequences?	*	*What:* Investigate threats; develop and communicate district policy. *Who:* Superintendent. *By when:* February 15.

*Highest-priority issue.

When we clarify, we ask questions such as, What do you mean by . . . ? What is important about this issue? What else about this bothers you? We ensure that everyone understands that issue and the other perspectives involved. Clarifying helps those who own the issue know they have been heard. When people know they have been heard, they can listen more easily. People's emotions may rise, and they may speak in more strident tones when they don't *believe* or *know* they've been heard. When we make the issues visible and clarify their meaning, we demonstrate to others that we have captured their issue, even if we have yet to address it.

Applying the Process: School Violence Example

After the issues have been listed, the group members further clarify each one by asking, What does each issue mean? What is important about this issue? Column 2 of Figure 6.1 shows how the group uses questions to help clarify the issues they have identified.

Assess Priorities

All issues are typically not equally important or urgent. Even though each issue identified is worthy of examination, we must determine what to work on first. In the first two steps of situation appraisal, we determine what we are dealing with. In this third step, we determine the order in which to consider the issues. We ask key questions such as, What issues are most important? What issues need to be addressed first?

To indicate priorities, we can use any way we want that makes sense to us and those we work with. Some people use an asterisk (*) to mark the highest-priority issues; others might want to use the terms "high," "medium," and "low." The purpose of this step is to get a clear picture of the relative priorities of the issues identified.

It is easy to believe that something critically important to us should be a top priority for everyone. Yet when we put the issues in order of priority within the context of all that must be dealt with, justifying how critical our concerns are may become harder. We need to factor in the concerns of others and the relative priorities of all the issues. Remember, even if an issue has a lower priority, we can't forget about it; we still need to address it. But if we know an issue has a lower priority, we can make better-informed decisions about resources and timing.

The actual priority a concern receives is often less important than the discussion that setting priorities generates. Inevitably, people disagree about some priorities, but everyone learns more or is forced to consider new ideas when they explain their rationale and advocate for one priority or another. The most important point about setting priorities is that clear priorities are indicated, and people reach consensus about those priorities.

Applying the Process: School Violence Example

The task force examines the long list of issues they have generated. Clearly, the members need to set priorities because the district does not have the resources to do everything at once. As a group, they determine the highest priorities. In Column 3 of Figure 6.1, the group identifies the highest-priority issues with an asterisk.

Before we explain what goes into Column 4 of Figure 6.1, we want to offer a suggestion for assessing the highest-priority issues we've identified. Sometimes we can make our priority setting more objective if we examine each issue in light of the following three dimensions:

- *Seriousness*. How serious or important is this issue? What is its effect (e.g., on people and cost)?
- *Urgency*. How quickly is action needed? What is the deadline?
- *Growth*. What is the trend? What if we do nothing? Will the problem get worse, get better, or stay the same?

We can rate each question's priority as "high," "medium," or "low." Issues may have a high priority in one dimension (e.g., urgency), but a low priority in another dimension (e.g., seriousness). When we look at all three dimensions, a greater range of priorities often results. Figure 6.2 shows how the school violence example would look if we set priorities using seriousness, urgency, and growth. Using these dimensions allows us to more clearly state our rationale for how we set a priority. Regardless of which priority-setting method we use, once we have assessed priorities, we continue on to the final step of situation appraisal: Name next steps.

Name Next Steps

After we bring issues to the surface, clarify them, and put them in order of priority, all is for naught if we do not act on what we have identified. Even though the purpose of situation appraisal is not to resolve issues, we do want to leave ourselves with a good idea of what to do next. In this step, we ask, What should be done next? By whom? By when? We should ask these questions of each issue we identify.

We have all participated in meetings where participants have a lot of good discussion, but the meeting ends and nothing ever happens. Action items are not identified, or if they are, no one is assigned to take action. Action items that are everyone's responsibility become no one's responsibility. If leaders do not specify who needs to do what, by when, probably nothing will happen. When we clarify what needs to be done, assign responsibility, and designate a due date, we maximize the chance that some action will be taken.

Sometimes the next step that makes the most sense is to use one of the four analytic tools to explore and resolve an issue. For example, we might need to decide how best to communicate a policy change or choose a new team leader. *Decision analysis* can help us decide. Maybe we need to determine why we have persistent, unanticipated budget shortfalls or why finding substitute teachers for certain schools is so difficult. *Problem analysis* can help us find the cause. If we need to implement a policy change or plan an upcoming event, *potential problem analysis* can help us. Sometimes we need to look further into an issue before we can decide how best to proceed. When we are not sure how to proceed, *situation appraisal* can help us separate and investigate an issue before we determine how to resolve it.

Applying the Process:
School Violence Example

Task force members develop an action plan for each major issue identified. They consider *what*

98

See the Issues	Clarify the Issues	Assess Priorities		
		Seriousness	Urgency	Growth
Safety precautions	What precautions are in place to screen for guns? How do we identify at-risk students? What can we learn from other districts' experiences? Are students and staff given emergency drills?	H	H	H
School uniforms	Are we going to have school uniforms? Are we going to limit individuals' freedom of expression?	M	M	L
Identification of staff, students, and visitors	How do we know who should and shouldn't be on school grounds? What is current district policy? Do we need a system of identification?	H	H	H
Upcoming prom	What do we know about tensions increasing between student cliques? What do we know about rumors of possible disturbance at the prom?	H	M	L
Recent threats	Where are they coming from? What's current policy? Do we need severe consequences?	H	H	H

FIGURE 6.2
Assessing Priorities in the School Violence Example

Note: H = high; M = medium; L = low.

exactly should be done to further address this issue, *who* will be responsible for any action (individual or group), and *when* the action should be completed. Several issues require more in-depth consideration by others—either individuals or task forces. Column 4 of Figure 6.1 shows the actions the task force identified.

Applying Situation Appraisal in Schools

Let's examine situations where administrators and teachers found situation appraisal worthwhile. First, we consider administrative applications of situation appraisal, and then we look at how it can be used with students.

Examples of Administrative Use

Examining a troublesome situation. A school improvement team at Scranton Middle School (Brighton, Michigan) identified parental and student concerns about busing to and from school. Behavior problems and a lack of civility had spilled over beyond busing times and encroached on the school day, thereby affecting the school community. The team set a goal to improve the level of respect between students and between students and staff. They gathered a group that represented all stakeholders—students, parents, teachers, administrators, bus drivers, and counselors. That group identified and clarified the issues at one meeting. At the next meeting, group members put the issues in order of priority and agreed which had the highest priority. They developed an action plan to increase communication among drivers, students, and parents and to empower the bus drivers to handle disturbing situations. Figure 6.3 shows sample results of their efforts.

Encouraging participation and understanding. Over several months in Orlando, Florida, tensions built within a middle school community. Numerous incidents and issues occurred involving the school, and parents lost confidence in the school's leadership. Emotions reached the boiling point. The district called a meeting for concerned parents and others. The

media were present. The district sent a team of people to facilitate the meeting. The team leader welcomed the 100 or so assembled people and introduced the proposed objectives and agenda for the evening.

The large group then broke into smaller groups to air issues and concerns. Because so many issues were listed, the facilitators asked groups to pick their highest-priority issues. The groups then spent time clarifying them. By setting priorities before they clarified the issues, the facilitators ensured that everyone's issues were elicited. Participants may get so involved explaining an emotional issue that other issues may never get aired. Clarifying a large number of issues, especially when emotion is involved and the time frame is limited, can be time-consuming. Figure 6.4 (p. 102) shows an excerpt of one group's work. Notice how thoroughly the high-priority issues have been clarified. Typically, issues such as lack of communication and safety have many interpretations and subelements. Clarification helps ensure clarity and increased understanding.

No action plan was developed during the meeting because the meeting's primary purpose was to give everyone present a chance to contribute and explain their concerns and points of view. The district set expectations: They would consider what steps to take and communicate these to the school community. People left the meeting believing they had been heard and that the district cared about what they had to say. The district had a much clearer idea of the nature of the issues at this school. In cases like this, if we provide an opportunity for people to vent their frustration and opinions, not only do we elicit valuable input for decision makers about the nature of a situation, but we also buy time so that administrators can take thoughtful

FIGURE 6.3
Situation Appraisal in the School Bus Example

Issue	Clarification of Issues	PRIORITY			Next Steps
		Seriousness	Urgency	Growth	
Mix of high school students with middle school students.	Swearing, age-appropriate language and comments, and vandalism.	H	H	M	1. Propose a new driver-empowered referral system for K–12.
Disruptive behavior, violence, teasing, and disciplinary write-ups.	Many disciplinary write-ups, mostly for middle school students picking on each other.	H	H	H	2. Increase driver training in the new system and student management techniques.
Relationships between students and bus drivers and lack of time for communication.	Training—No consistency in driver expectation. Lack of bus driver empowerment to enforce discipline.	H	H	H	
Driver shortage.	Overcrowded buses (three students per seat). Unwillingness of high school students to share seats. Driver shortage and lack of skills. Inconsistency of driver assignments.	M+	M+	H	3. Keep equipment and driver recruitment issues before the board and public
Additional training for drivers—including student behavior management.	More training needed for some drivers. Not enough assertive discipline. Disrespectful student behavior toward drivers (more than toward teachers and administrators). Lack of student consequences.	H	H	H	
Equipment (buses and video equipment).	Should video or other equipment be added to buses?	H	H	M	

Note: H = high; M = medium; L = low.

101

FIGURE 6.4
Flexible Use of Situation Appraisal

Issue	Priority	Clarification of Issues
Homework	*	Inconsistency among teachers in amount given (some too much, some too little).
		Does not fit rationale given for block schedule (homework was to be done in school during block).
Lack of communication	*	Little communication from school to parents on important issues.
		Late or delayed communication to parents.
		Phone calls from parents not returned by staff in a timely manner.
		Inadequate communication on homework.
		Too many layers in communication process.
		Parents not notified when teachers are leaving.
		No newsletter informing parents about school activities.
Field trips		Often canceled.
Safety	*	Lack of discipline by teachers and parents.
		Lack of consequences.
		Too much fighting; too many drugs and weapons.
		Lack of discipline in the cafeteria.
		Intimidation between students.
		Bus stops too far from home to leave student alone (one student at stop).
		Unsafe bus stop at school on Brooks Avenue.
		Staff not responding to student intimidation.
Truancy		High absenteeism.
		Inaccurate data or record keeping—students reported absent when they aren't.
Meeting times for parents		Times not conducive to family needs.
Not taking home books		
Quality of substitutes		

*Highest priority.

and appropriate action, rather than implement knee-jerk solutions.

Creating a process to handle conflicts. A concerned parent formally challenged the Laguna Beach Unified School District (California) about a piece of required reading. The parent wanted the book pulled from the 9th grade reading list because he believed the book projected antireligious stereotypes. He was an influential member of the community and had the support of like-minded parents. The district was concerned about the precedent the handling of this issue might set. They had no process in place to respond to a formal challenge, because they had never been challenged. The English Department had used the book successfully for years. In fact, it was on the state's recommended reading list. District officials created a textbook review committee of parents, teachers, students, and staff; they decided to use situation appraisal to air and put the concerns in order of priority. The parent who filed the challenge was asked to outline his concerns about the book. Here are some of them:

• Use of a book with religious themes was taught in a public school.
• The book contained excessive profanity.
• Parents were not informed of the book's content.
• Teachers did not choose a book that extolled the virtues of faith; rather, the book derided it.
• The book promoted the occult.
• The book's theme of hopelessness and futility was inappropriate in an era of teen suicide and feelings of despair in many teenagers.

• The book used extreme and graphic violence.

The English teacher was asked to respond to each concern. Both the parent and the teacher were asked to present their issues to the textbook review committee. After the committee members heard both sides of the issues, they put the concerns in order of priority, using their perception of the validity of making changes around a particular issue as a basis. They believed the following issues seemed to be most in need of action:

• Informing parents about what their children were reading.
• Excessive profanity in the book.
• The book's theme of hopelessness and futility.

The committee decided to keep the book in question as part of the core reading for 9th grade students. But it compiled suggestions for the English Department to better recognize potentially questionable material and better prepare parents and students. The district outlined and communicated a new general procedure for handling curriculum material that had been challenged. The steps incorporated elements of situation appraisal to arrive at a final recommendation.

The parent later wrote that although he wished the outcome had been different, he appreciated the professionalism and thoroughness of the district's response to his concerns. The district learned it could successfully mediate conflict-laden situations by using a process that dignifies and accounts for opinions on all sides of the issues.

Other administrative examples. Many other circumstances exist in which situation appraisal can be used. Here are examples:

• A new state school accountability program mandated Lowry Middle School (Ascension Parish, Louisiana) to develop a school improvement plan. School officials used situation appraisal to develop a plan they submitted to the Louisiana State Department of Education. Their plan was not only accepted, it became the model for all improvement plans in Louisiana.

• Dozens of schools within a school district had implemented a new reading program. The results were mixed. The software and materials were difficult to work with, but the students loved the program and were engaged in learning. A team used situation appraisal to identify the exact nature of district concerns and possible next steps. Team members raised specific issues to communicate to the software vendor. They identified several actions to help teachers use the materials more effectively and easily.

• Individuals in a district office outlined the skills required for success in various office support jobs. Incumbents completed individual situation appraisals of their concerns about these skills. Then they helped develop action plans to develop the skills they needed to excel in their jobs.

• A high school principal in Warren County, New Jersey, backed off from advocating a specific scheduling system for his high school. Instead, he asked his staff to identify, clarify, and put their concerns in order of priority. Once the principal better understood others' issues, he could more effectively develop a satisfactory solution.

• A team at an elementary school used situation appraisal to identify how members could better serve the increasing number of English as a Second Language (ESL) students. Team members then incorporated these issues into the overall ESL plan.

• A school administrator starts every monthly staff meeting with a situation appraisal as a way of taking the pulse of what's happening. Having everyone share their issues and concerns ensures that she and others are aware of what is happening and that the opportunity exists to resolve issues closer to their inception.

Examples of Classroom Use

Substance abuse and other realities. Laguna Beach High School (Laguna Beach, California) is hosting a substance abuse night to encourage dialogue within families about choices involving friendships, alcohol abuse, drugs, sex, and parties. More than 80 parents and students are gathered. Two high school teachers lead the session. They organize groups of five or six participants; the only rule is that students can't be in a group with their own parents. The leaders have developed short scenarios based on actual situations that involve Laguna Beach students (names, of course, have been changed). The scenarios deal with events such as a student having a party when his parents are away, parents getting a call from the police who have just arrested their child for driving under the influence, a student discovering a friend's boyfriend has hit her friend, a student who believes a friend has been drinking too much, and a friend at school who shows a classmate a gun in his locker. The facilitators lead the groups through situation appraisal by asking the process questions and

FIGURE 6.5
Situation Appraisal in the Substance Abuse Example

See the Issues	Clarify the Issues	Assess Priorities			Name Next Steps (Action Plan)
		Seriousness	Urgency	Growth	
Getting home safely	How do they get home? No license. No ride.	H	H	H	1. Find her friend and make sure she's okay.
Getting in trouble	Girls lied to parents.	L	M	H	2. Call her parents or a cab.
Her friend	How drunk is she? Does she need medical help? Can she take care of herself? Does she have a drinking problem?	H	H	H	3. Go pick up the car the next day.
The car	What should they do with her car?	M	L	H	
Not knowing anyone at the party	She's insecure. She's afraid to ask for help.	M	M	L	

Note: H = high; M = medium; L = low.

asking group members to record the answers on flip charts.

One scenario deals with two underage girls who drive 25 miles to a party after telling their parents they are going to the movies. The girl who has a driver's license gets drunk at the party. The other (the girl without a license) is left to figure out how to handle the situation. Figure 6.5 shows one group's work on this scenario, which looks at the situation from the perspective of the girl who doesn't have a license.

All the groups have substantive and lively discussions. At the end of the evening, students and parents are asked to provide feedback. Here are some of their comments:

Student comments
The substance abuse night with our parents was a good way to make the point about alcohol and drugs on our campus. Most parents don't believe we have these problems. As a matter of fact, they are in a state of denial. When you understand there is a problem, it'll get fixed faster.

I didn't go to the substance abuse night to have fun, but working with other parents *was* fun.

More important, I really believe we communicated. I learned that telling my parents the truth was the best way to solve the problem.

My group, especially we students, learned how tough it is to be a parent.

Parents learned that grounding a kid doesn't necessarily solve a problem. Things are more complicated and deeper than we think.

It was nice having adults listen for once, instead of knowing all the answers. Like one parent in the group said, "I never knew you guys thought about these things."

Parent comments
I learned to appreciate my son—and his friends—a lot more. I forgot that they can think and they know what to do when given a chance.

I realized how important kids' opinions are.

It is hard to believe that kids abuse substances, are date raped, and get addicted; perhaps I just didn't want to believe it. Well, now I do.

Communication is the blockade between my daughter and me, and this may bridge a tremendous gap.

Situation appraisal provides a vehicle through which people can express their opinions *and* listen to others' opinions. Hearing and being heard builds understanding. And understanding can lead to meaningful solutions.

Developing an understanding of different points of view. Eighth grade students at Thurston Middle School (Laguna Beach, California) are studying the end of the Civil War. Typically, students find that understanding the enormous implications of Reconstruction and how various groups of people were affected is difficult. A teacher can lecture about the effect of Reconstruction on southern soldiers, northern soldiers, southern women, and freed blacks, but then the list of issues and problems each group faced becomes little more than a list to memorize for a test.

So that his students can see things from different points of view, one teacher divides his class into four teams, each representing a different group of people. He sets the stage by reviewing Reconstruction in the South, the Homestead Act of 1862, and the industrialization of the North. He asks each team to picture its group at the end of the Civil War. Each team reads a short scenario developed for its population and uses the situation appraisal steps (SCAN) to identify and assess priorities and possible action plans from the vantage point of the group it represents.

Team members report their findings to the full class. Each team learns to better appreciate the perspective of its own group as well as the perspectives of the other populations. The lesson provides a basis for understanding the actions and societal changes that followed the Civil War. Suddenly, events that seemed inexplicable make sense when viewed from a given perspective. The perspectives that students develop from this lesson provide a foundation as they move forward with their study of U.S. history.

Understanding complicated themes. A middle school social studies teacher in a large urban district prepares to present a unit on the Revolutionary War. She asks her students to imagine their state has decided it is sick of the way the United States government treats it. Most of the state's citizens have voted to secede from the United States and create their own country. The teacher asks the students to break into groups, list, and clarify the concerns they would have as citizens of this new country. Here are some of their concerns:

- Laws. What laws will we have?
- Government. What form of government will we use?
- Currency. What money will we use?
- Safety. How will we protect ourselves? How will we build our own army?
- Reactions. How will the rest of the country react?
- Dissent. What do we do about the state citizens who didn't want to secede?
- Name. What will we call ourselves?
- Credibility. Will other countries take us seriously?
- Food supply. How will we feed our people?
- Taxes. How will we raise money?

The teams assess priorities and develop simple action plans based on their high-priority issues. The teacher uses the results of this lesson to begin discussion about the Revolution and the realities America faced in breaking away from its mother country. By bringing the situation closer to home, she makes it easier for students to make the connection to 200 years ago.

The teacher later presents the work to fellow teachers who marvel at the high quality of the students' answers. When asked if she had one of the gifted classes, she replies that she has the same students that everyone else has (there are only two students even designated as gifted in her school of 1,100). She says, "I realized that after all my years of teaching, I have been underestimating the thinking ability of my students."

Other student examples. Many situations exist in which students can use situation appraisal. Here are examples:

- A Mt. Olive (New Jersey) science teacher uses situation appraisal as she begins a unit on space travel. She sets the stage by announcing that NASA is launching a Kids in Space program, and this class will determine who should go. Students watch the movie *Apollo 13* and write down their concerns about space travel and kids in space. After the movie, groups clarify the issues and choose the most critical ones. The issues they listed help the teacher see what understanding and misconceptions exist about space travel. The students begin to gain ownership for the learning. As the unit continues over the next couple of days, students apply decision analysis to select actual students for the hypothetical program and protect those decisions by doing potential problem analysis.
- Students of a physical education teacher at John Witherspoon Middle School (Princeton, New Jersey) do a situation appraisal on a new exercise program. The students are setting up exercise programs for themselves. They consider their concerns about the program and identify what they need to do (action plan) to help make it successful.
- Female students approach a high school guidance counselor and ask for help working through a situation appraisal. They are concerned

that a friend may be suicidal, and they are unsure of what to do. The counselor helps them identify and clarify their issues and questions. The girls assess priorities and develop a simple action plan. They determine that they need to express their concern to their friend and tell her why they needed to share their concern with the guidance counselor. They suggest that their friend talk with her parents and the guidance counselor.

• A middle school social science teacher at Whitman Middle School (Wauwatosa, Wisconsin) uses situation appraisal before a group project. Class members discuss their concerns about group projects and what makes such projects difficult. They identify the biggest issue. Their action plan becomes a list of do's and don'ts that they agree to abide by when they work on team projects (e.g., don't make fun of people in your group, treat each other with respect, encourage participation, and don't tell anyone to shut up).

• Seventh grade students at Scranton Middle School (Brighton, Michigan) are starting a unit on eating disorders and their effect on teenagers. The class divides into four groups: parents, friends, classmates, and anorexics. Each group lists the issues they believe surround anorexia. The action plans become ways group members could help the anorexic.

• Elementary school students are beginning a unit on the theme of survival. They will read several books in which the need for survival plays a large role. Before they start the unit, their teacher reads them the opening of the fairytale "Hansel and Gretel," in which the father leaves his children alone in the woods because he can't afford to feed them. The students list and clarify issues, assess priorities (using smiley faces), and develop a simple action plan.

Many of the same issues Hansel and Gretel had to consider will surface as the students move through the unit's readings.

Situation appraisal can help us more effectively and thoroughly understand and examine difficult and complex situations. We can use the process alone and with others. It helps us gather and use the input of stakeholders. Too often, people tend to shy away from difficult situations because they are afraid of conflict or of involving others. Without a process to follow, complexity and conflict can lead us astray. Situation appraisal, however, like a road map, can help us find our way through the maze of complicated situations.

In the classroom, situation appraisal can help students better understand the intricacies and realities of complex issues or concepts. This tool helps encourage students to consider alternate perspectives. Different views help students see the elements of a situation in light of reality. The framework of situation appraisal also helps students organize their thinking while they consider many issues.

Like any effective approach, situation appraisal is flexible enough to accommodate a range of situations. Once we understand how to use situation appraisal, we can modify it to fit the needs of an individual situation. For example, *how* we indicate priorities (using an asterisk; a designation of "high," "medium," and "low"; arrows; or smiley faces) is not as important as making sure that somehow we indicate priorities—if prioritization is what the situation calls for. Perhaps all we want to do is air the issues and give a voice to stakeholders. In that case, assigning priorities may be less important than ensuring issues are listed and clarified.

If situations are clear-cut, we may not need to use situation appraisal. Perhaps another analytic tool would be more useful (e.g., decision analysis, problem analysis, or potential problem analysis). Yet all too often, life's most important challenges are messy, especially when multiple stakeholders, issues, opinions, and consequences are involved. Situation appraisal helps us see and hear more clearly. We are capable of better solutions when we better understand what we are dealing with.

< 7 >

Getting Started

All glory comes from daring to begin.

—ANONYMOUS

Learning about the analytic tools presented in this book is an important first step to making them work for us. To ultimately realize the benefits they can create, however, we have to use them. An idea that isn't used changes nothing.

We hope we have convinced you to think about alternative ways to resolve thorny issues. Perhaps we have helped give a name or provide a framework to what you already do well. Or maybe we have helped you see ways to do things even better. What counts most is if and how these ideas end up helping you and others.

In this chapter, we suggest ways to help you get started. We introduce three different ways to use an analytic process: to resolve a single issue, to improve operations, and to help students in the classroom. For each use, we explain the stages and provide a scenario to show how you might apply them. We consider how the purposes may differ in each use, or approach, how rational process fits in, and what comes next.

Before examining each approach, we want to discuss two topics that may influence how a rational process is used in each approach. First, we look at how the four analytic processes interrelate: A natural connection exists between them. Next, we talk about the various levels of complexity with which we might use a single process. Out of necessity, we introduce each process in its entirety; in practice, this is not representative of how each process is often used. Frequently, a single step or a combination of steps may be sufficient to accomplish what a situation demands. The use of each process is flexible and is driven by the needs of a given issue.

How the Processes Interrelate

Each rational process has value and usefulness in its own right. As you may have suspected, however, there is a logical flow to how the processes might be connected. Consider the following: Central High School is in a panic because it is opening week and 150 more students appeared than were projected by the enrollment figures that the school was given. To help them identify and sort through the concerns, educators can use situation appraisal as soon as they discover the extra students. The school was already at full capacity before the extra students showed up. How could the projections be so far off? Certainly this is a deviation: The actual number of students exceeds the expected number of students. We do not know why the projections were wrong. Do we need to know the cause? We need to figure out what to do about the extra students. But finding the cause might also prevent the problem from occurring again or happening elsewhere. It makes sense to use problem analysis.

In the meantime, Central's teachers and administrators need to decide how to handle the extra students. One or more decisions need to be made. Surely, decision analysis applies. Note that we are making decisions to take Band-Aid actions. We haven't yet found the cause of the problem, but we need to take action anyway. Once the cause of the problem is found, administrators can use decision analysis again to decide what cor-

rective action to take. Perhaps the cause is a software glitch or an administrative process that failed to provide certain checks and balances. Whatever the cause, administrators will need to decide how to eliminate it.

After they have used decision analysis to decide how to handle the problem, they need to implement their solution. Perhaps they have decided to relocate some students to a nearby school with more space. To handle the remaining students, they will have to increase the average class size and use portable classrooms. They can use potential problem analysis to ensure they successfully implement these various actions. Potential problem analysis helps identify the problems that could arise around implementing the solution and shows how best to prevent and handle any future problems. Once we implement the solution, more deviations may occur, and the cycle begins again.

Situation appraisal is a different case. It helps us see the need to apply problem analysis to find the true cause, to use decision analysis to figure out short-term and longer-term solutions, and to use potential problem analysis to take action and implement change. Situation appraisal can also be useful at any point during the cycle. Sometimes we need to get others involved and let them air their concerns, though not necessarily resolve those concerns. Sometimes we just need to take stock of what is happening. At other times, we need to further separate a complicated issue to identify a specific issue (e.g., decision, plan, or deviation) to work on. Sometimes we're not sure what to do next; we need to examine the issue or circumstance in greater depth. Situation appraisal applies to all these situations. Situation appraisal is almost like an umbrella process that can steer us toward any or each of the other three analytic processes (problem

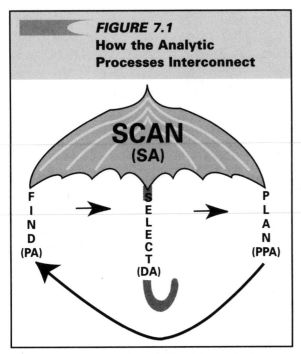

FIGURE 7.1
How the Analytic Processes Interconnect

SCAN
(SA)

F
I
N
D
(PA)

S
E
L
E
C
T
(DA)

P
L
A
N
(PPA)

Note: SA = situation appraisal; PA = problem analysis; DA = decision analysis; PPA = potential problem analysis.

analysis, decision analysis, or potential problem analysis). When in doubt, we can always use situation appraisal. In addition, we may need it at any point during the issue-resolution cycle. Figure 7.1 shows how this interconnection between the processes might look.

How Much of a Process Do We Need to Use?

In the preceding chapters, we introduced each analytic process in its entirety. But actual situations may not require a complete use (i.e., all steps and refinements) of a particular process. Usually, in fact, one step or a couple of steps may be all that's required to meet the needs of a situation. Consider a meeting with a student's angry parents. The first two steps of situation appraisal

("see the issues" and "clarify the issues") may be sufficient. Completing all four steps might be overkill. Or maybe a student is considering dropping out of school. If you help the student think through the risks associated with that decision (i.e., using only the "consider risks" step of decision analysis) the student can see the consequences of his choice before he makes it. These are examples of single idea or bits-and-pieces use.

Other situations may demand using only the basic steps of a process. Imagine the following occurrence: Two teachers approach a high school principal and ask her to authorize a workshop on classroom discipline at an upcoming inservice day. The principal assesses their recommendation. She hasn't been privy to their discussions, and she wants to test the process they used. She asks the teachers these questions: "What were your objectives?" "What other options did you consider?" "How did the options compare to your objectives?" "What are the primary risks associated with offering this workshop?" "Why did you ultimately select this particular workshop?" In a few short questions, the principal has used most of the core steps of decision analysis. She did not have to write the process down or perform a complicated analysis with several different people. She was able to effectively test their recommendation just by asking good questions. The principal was able to see how well they had thought through their decision.

Occasionally, a situation requires a more complete use of a process—all the steps and refinements. Consider a district facilities manager who is wrestling with a vexing problem. A recent inventory shows that large numbers of inventory items are missing. Where are the missing items? How have they gotten out of the building? The manager decides to use problem analysis to determine the cause of the problem. When he needs more information, he makes a phone call or asks a colleague to look at what he is learning about the situation. On his way to finding the cause, he completes all steps of problem analysis, including distinctions and changes. The refinements provide some important clues to the mysterious disappearance of inventoried items.

In our experience, a single step or two is sufficient use of a process to meet the needs of a situation approximately 80 percent of the time. About 15 percent of the time, the basic steps are enough to reach the necessary conclusion. Only about 5 percent of the time do we need to use all the steps and refinements.

We choose how much of a process to use by knowing what end result we are looking for. Do we need to make a decision? Then we may want to use the basic steps or full steps of decision analysis. If we are just trying to set some goals, the step "establish and classify objectives" will be sufficient. Or perhaps our students have difficulty recognizing they have decisions and choices to make. The first step of decision analysis, "state the decision," might meet the need. We find it easy to think of a step only in conjunction with its fellow steps. But this outlook underestimates the value a single step can add to a situation. By knowing what kind of conclusion or result is required, we can better know which process and which steps will achieve that result. As with any new skill or tool, the more comfortable and knowledgeable we are about it, the more we can use it flexibly and simply when necessary.

Reasons to Use an Analytic Process

As explained earlier in the chapter, we examine three major ways, or reasons, to apply a rational process: to resolve a single issue, to improve operations, and to help students in the classroom. Each reason has a series of stages we might move toward to accomplish our purpose (see Figure 7.2 on p. 114). As the figure shows, regardless of the reason for using a process, three major phases exist for each approach: planning, implementing, and evaluating results.

Of course, not every issue requires this thorough planning and preparation. These approaches are mapped out as suggestions for how a process might be applied for each of three major purposes. We encourage you to jump in and use a process; there are not many ways to really mess it up! For those of us who like to think things through before doing, we hope these approaches will provide a road map.

Single-Issue Resolution

We might want to use an analytic process to resolve a single issue. Single-issue resolution has five stages: Determine desired result, identify process, plan for process use, implement plan, and assess results. To translate the stages into action, we use a scenario.

A scenario for single-issue resolution. A school district is facing severe budget problems. The athletic director has been asked to make a recommendation to the school board about which athletic teams should be cut next year to accommodate the new budget. He is in an unenviable position, but he needs to reach a conclusion and then present his recommendation.

Determine desired result. What are we trying to do? Are we trying to

- Make a decision? A recommendation?
- Find out why something went wrong?

113

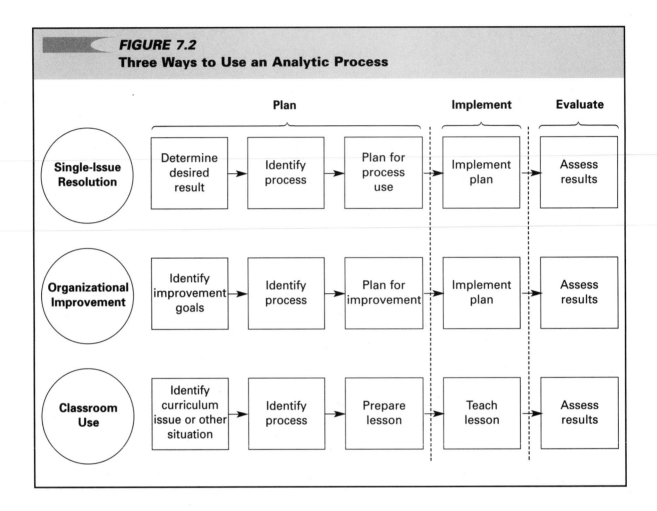

FIGURE 7.2
Three Ways to Use an Analytic Process

	Plan			Implement	Evaluate
Single-Issue Resolution	Determine desired result	Identify process	Plan for process use	Implement plan	Assess results
Organizational Improvement	Identify improvement goals	Identify process	Plan for improvement	Implement plan	Assess results
Classroom Use	Identify curriculum issue or other situation	Identify process	Prepare lesson	Teach lesson	Assess results

• Implement a plan, change, or decision that's been made?

• Sort through a messy or complicated issue? Figure out what to do next?

Applying the Process: Budget Cut Example

The athletic director has been asked to submit a recommendation. He needs to decide which teams to cut.

Identify process. We need to match the most appropriate tool or process for the job with the desired end result. What are we trying to do? Are we trying to

• Make a decision? A recommendation? Use decision analysis.

• Find out why something went wrong? Use problem analysis.

• Implement a plan, change, or decision that's been made? Use potential problem analysis.

• Sort through a messy or complicated issue? Use situation appraisal.

We need to consider how much of the process to use. Should we use all process steps, or will a single step accomplish what we need? For example, we might want to use only the first problem analysis step, "focus on the problem," if we are trying to pinpoint the biggest problems our district is experiencing. Simply listing the deviations helps us get a bigger picture. Later on, we might want to select some of these deviations to apply problem analysis to.

Applying the Process:
Budget Cut Example

The athletic director determines that because he must make a choice about which sports teams to cut, he will use decision analysis. He decides to use the full process because his decision is critical and involves many stakeholders.

Plan for process use. We need to ask ourselves some questions:

• What needs to be done to accomplish each step?
• Who needs to be involved at each step? Who has needed information? Who will have ultimate responsibility for completing the step?
• By when will we want each step accomplished?
• What needs to happen with the conclusion? Who needs to see or approve it? In what form should we present it (if any)?

Applying the Process:
Budget Cut Example

The athletic director puts together a simple plan, shown in Figure 7.3.

FIGURE 7.3
Athletic Director's "Plan for Process Use" in the Budget Cut Decision

What	Who	By When
State the decision; establish and classify objectives, including weights.	Me. With input from coaches, athletes, parents, and staff.	April 15.
List alternatives (existing teams) and evaluate (score) alternatives.	Me.	April 30.
Consider risks.	Me. Talk with other districts that have cut programs.	May 7.
Trust your work—pick a winner!	Me.	May 9.
Prepare a recommendation for presentation.	Me.	May 15.

115

Implement plan. Here we actually carry out the plan for using the process that we identified in the previous steps. Along the way, issues may surface that need further attention. We may want to make note of these so we can address them later. Modifying or adjusting our plan may be necessary to accommodate changing circumstances or issues. If we know what we are trying to accomplish (Step 1) we can keep focused on the overall goal as we make the necessary adjustments.

Applying the Process:
Budget Cut Example

The athletic director carries out the steps in his plan (see Figure 7.3). Because he has clearly identified each step, the people who need to be involved, and the date when each step needs to be completed, he is prepared to move forward. Although implementation may not go exactly as anticipated, up-front planning generally helps the process go more smoothly.

Assess results. Once the analysis is complete and the conclusion is reached, we need to determine what next steps are required. Consider the following questions:

• What lessons did we learn from this experience? What could we have done better or differently? What worked particularly well?
• What do we need to do next to ensure success?
• Whom do we need to share the results of the analysis with? What form should this communication take?

Applying the Process:
Budget Cut Example

After he presents the recommendation to the board, the athletic director realizes he could have strengthened his analysis and conclusion by having a team of people work with him. If he had the task to do over again, he would appoint a team consisting of athletes, coaches, and parents to help make this important decision. The people on the team could talk to their peers and represent those groups of stakeholders. Of course, someone is always going to be unhappy with the results of a decision such as the athletic director had to make. A team, however, would ensure that all groups are represented and that the recommendation will more likely be supported.

Organizational Improvement

We can also use an analytic process to achieve the following:

• Improve the way we approach repetitive types of situations (e.g., meetings and hiring decisions).
• Accomplish a specific district or school goal (e.g., include community and stakeholders in important decisions and implement district philosophy).

We look at what we might do at each stage of using an analytic process for organizational improvement. Here are the stages: identify improvement goals, identify process, plan for improvement, implement plan, and assess results. We use a typical organizational improvement situation to illustrate how each stage might look.

A scenario for organizational improvement. The situation involves a large school district. The assistant superintendent in charge of administration believes meetings could be run more effectively. Her suspicions have been confirmed. A recent survey of district personnel identified their biggest complaints as the overabundance of meetings and the ineffective use of meeting time. The survey pinpointed some meeting problems:

- There are too many meetings.
- The purpose of the meetings is unclear and not adhered to.
- Key people are not at the meetings—others are not sure why they *are* present.
- Little of substance seems to be accomplished during meetings.
- Meetings drag on—they are too long.
- Meetings have to be continued at another time, and then participants go over the same ground at subsequent meetings.
- It is not clear who is responsible for doing things after meetings; consequently, little is done.

Identify improvement goals. Consider the following questions:

- What kinds of improvements would we like to see in people, systems, and procedures?
- Where within the district or school would we most like to improve relationships or people's abilities to work together?
- In what ways are goals or objectives not being achieved?
- What key initiatives need to be successfully implemented?
- What problems tend to occur or recur?
- What changes in people's perceptions of the district or school would we most like to see?

- Two years from now, what do we see as the biggest challenges facing this school or district?

The answers to these questions help us identify the desired organizational results that an analytic process can address.

Applying the Process: Effective Meetings Example

The assistant superintendent believes using a rational process can ensure that meeting time is effective and efficient. She sets goals for meetings. Here is what meetings should have:

- A clear purpose and objectives.
- A designated start and end time.
- A proposed agenda.
- The right people involved.
- A time at the beginning or end for participants to air their concerns.
- A clear action plan for next steps.
- A clear process to follow.

Identify process. To achieve the goals we have identified, we need to determine which process or processes would most help us and how we want to use them. Please refer to the "identify process" stage in the Single-Issue Resolution section given earlier in the chapter.

Applying the Process: Effective Meetings Example

The assistant superintendent has determined that decision analysis and situation appraisal would probably be the most help to improve meetings within the district. She believes that using one step of decision analysis, "establish and classify objectives," will ensure that each meeting has clearly stated objectives and that these objectives are identified as items that must be accomplished or items that would be nice to accomplish if time and opportunity permit. She believes these objectives will provide focus to meetings and agendas. A lot of meeting time is spent sharing concerns and issues, without having an organized way to capture them. Therefore, she wants to use all steps of situation appraisal when appropriate. Sometimes even the first step, "see the issues," will help everyone feel they have had a chance to share what is on their mind and that these issues are captured.

The assistant superintendent also wants all meetings to end by using the principles in "name next steps." Each issue and action item should be clearly identified, list a target completion date, and designate a person to be responsible for it.

Plan for improvement. In this stage, we plan how to achieve the goals we set in the previous step. We consider several questions:

• *Who should acquire the skills?* Who needs exposure to these tools or processes for the district or school to achieve the goals?
• *How can we introduce these skills?* How can we best introduce them to people?
• *How can we prepare the environment?* How can we ensure the most supportive environment for using these skills?
• *What needs to be done?* What, specifically, do we need to do to achieve the goals?

Who should acquire the skills? Consider who needs to do things differently to achieve the goals we identified in the previous stage. Whose

support or commitment do we need to successfully reach our goal?

How can we introduce these skills? Once we identify what we want to accomplish, which analytic skills will best help us reach that goal, and who needs the skills, we need to determine how to transfer or introduce the skills. Here are some options:

• *Modeling.* Rather than teach the skills, someone who has had exposure to the skills begins to use them. This procedure sets a powerful example and demonstrates the value of the tools in given situations. Rather than legislating use of the skills, modeling helps others acquire motivation to learn them.
• *Coaching.* Working with others individually or in small groups shows them how analytic processes might help them resolve issues or do certain things more effectively.
• *Integrating.* These skills can be integrated into the normal procedures and systems of an organization and can thus transfer to others. For example, hiring requests might require a list of objectives (including *musts* and *wants*) that a candidate must meet. Other districts have required that recommendations be submitted in a modified decision analysis format. Even if people have not been exposed to decision analysis, they can be encouraged to identify the objectives they considered in choosing an alternative, list the alternatives they considered, and highlight associated risks. This approach can be used with any of the other means of introducing the skills.
• *Teaching individuals.* For districts or sites that want a more in-depth exposure to these skills, a workshop can help individuals learn these processes and apply them to education-based cases and to actual school and classroom situations that participants identify. The concept

briefings, group practice, and instructor feedback ensure that participants leave class capable of using all these tools in real-life situations and in the classroom.

• *Using in-house capability.* Program leaders can be certified to teach these skills within their own districts. Certification helps districts or sites develop their own resource people, capable of delivering these skills internally. This is a cost-effective and beneficial option for districts that want a large number of people able to use these skills. An advantage to this approach is that a district has an in-house process expert who is familiar with the operations and issues that face the district and who is on site and available to help address or facilitate resolution of district issues.

Applying the Process: Effective Meetings Example

The assistant superintendent determines that the people who could most benefit from using these skills are those who are most likely to conduct meetings: department heads, school principals, and project leaders. The assistant superintendent is the only one familiar with these tools. Therefore, she decides to start slowly and build some enthusiasm for using them. She makes a commitment that she will *model* the use of these skills within the meetings she runs, and she will *coach* people who report directly to her in how to use some of the ideas in the meetings they run. If and when interest and enthusiasm for the skills grow, then she will perhaps authorize a workshop for her staff.

How can we prepare the environment? Our experience has shown that to successfully use these ideas to change how issues are addressed and how organizations are run, the work environment must support use of these skills. Organizations that see the greatest benefit from these skills are those where the following statements are true:

• Expectations for using these skills are clearly identified through goals and objectives. If the district wants to use these processes to help implement a particular strategic objective, for example, the link is clearly stated.
• People have the ability not only to recognize when to use the tools but to apply them in the desired ways.
• Efforts to use the skills are rewarded.
• Feedback and support regarding use of the skills are provided.
• People are allowed to practice, refine, and extend use of the skills.

What needs to be done? To have an effective action plan, we need to determine specifically what needs to be done, who will make sure it gets done, and when it needs to be accomplished. We want to consider the answers we have developed to the plan for improvement (i.e., Who should acquire the skills? How can we introduce these skills?).

Implement plan. Here we carry out the plan we developed. As we move along, we undoubtedly will need to make modifications and adjustments and note issues that may need further attention.

Applying the Process: Effective Meetings Example

Our assistant superintendent develops the action plan shown in Figure 7.4 (p. 120).

Assess results. We ask others and our-selves these questions:

- How well have we achieved our goals or desired results?
- What prevented us from achieving them or from achieving more?
- What actions can we take to address these barriers?
- What can we do to sustain and build upon our successes?
- Do we need to set new goals and begin the cycle again on new issues?

Applying the Process:
Effective Meetings Example

After the first three months of trying this new approach to meetings, the assistant superintendent assembles those who report directly to her and de-briefs them. These people report they are getting much better feedback about the meetings they run. They also spend less time in meetings. Unfortu-nately, they don't feel completely confident about their ability to facilitate contentious issues. The as-sistant superintendent makes note that this may be a future staff development opportunity. The people who report to her suggest distributing meeting ob-jectives and agendas ahead of time to help people better prepare. As a group, they agree to carry out this suggestion for subsequent meetings.

Classroom Use

Teachers who use these analytic tools within their classrooms and in dealing with stu-dents in other situations report that the students have developed the following skills:

FIGURE 7.4
Assistant Superintendent's Plan for Improvement in the Effective Meetings Example

What	Who	By When
Meet with those who report directly to me. Share survey results and improvement goals.	Me.	Next week.
Model use of meeting expectations and analytic process during meetings, as applicable.	Me.	Ongoing.
Encourage those who attempt to use these skills in the meetings they run.	Me.	Ongoing.
Solicit and provide feedback and support on how meetings are going.	Others and me.	Ongoing—formally, within three months.
Consider additional staff development if warranted or requested.	Me.	After three months.

• Display better questioning techniques in gathering, organizing, and evaluating information.

• Develop greater ability to resolve real-life problems.

• Gain greater understanding of curriculum material.

• Improve their ability to work in groups.

• Give better, more structured, and coherent presentations.

• Are more involved in and excited about learning.

• Learn problem-solving approaches they can apply to their own situations.

Teachers report that, once mastered, these tools have the following results:

• Helps make more effective use of longer class periods.

• Is a proven way to integrate higher-order thinking skills into the existing curriculum.

• Provides opportunities for continual assessment of student learning.

• Is energizing as teachers see the students' involvement and enthusiasm.

• Can actually shorten the necessary lesson preparation time.

• Helps teachers facilitate more than lecture.

Let us examine the stages to use these tools in the classroom: identify curriculum issue or other situation, identify process, prepare lesson, teach lesson, and assess results. A scenario shows how they apply.

A scenario for classroom use. A middle school health teacher is completing a unit on eating disorders. She finds an article about a 14-year-old girl who is 5 feet, 5 inches tall and weighs 90 pounds. The girl believes she is fat and has decided to go on a diet. The health teacher thinks this article might be an ideal opportunity to apply a rational process.

Identify curriculum issue or other situation. Issues that students face in real life are ideal candidates for introducing the analytic tools. Consider

• A decision they have to make.

• An upcoming change. A plan or action that needs to be implemented.

• Something that has gone unexpectedly wrong.

• A difficult and complicated issue that is tough to sort out and know how to proceed.

Students can also use these tools to help think about curriculum material in a new way. Figure 7.5 (p. 122) shows questions to stimulate your thinking about where in the curriculum you could use these analytic processes.

Applying the Process:
Eating Disorders Example

The teacher is aware that many of her students know someone who struggles with a possible eating disorder. She determines that this relevant and difficult issue is worth closer examination.

Identify process. In the previous stage, we identified a situation in which a tool might apply. Now we have to determine which process would be the greatest help and how much of that process we need to

FIGURE 7.5

Identifying Where in the Curriculum an Analytic Process Might Apply

Situation or Issue	Questions to Think About
Decisions of others	What objectives (spoken or unspoken) may have motivated the decision makers?
	What might have been the priority of the objectives?
	What risks were associated with the various options (regardless of whether these risks were considered)?
	What did the decision makers ultimately decide?
Plans or changes initiated by others	What potential problems did they identify in advance? Which took them by surprise? Or what potential problems might they experience?
	What might cause those potential problems?
	What preventive actions did they identify in advance? Or what preventive actions might they take?
	What contingent actions had they prepared? Or what contingent actions might they be ready to take?
Deviations—what actually happened was different from what was expected to happen	How is the problem or deviation defined—what were the specific expectations? What actually happened?
	How would you describe the problem (both in terms of what actually happened [*is* information] and what did not happen but you might have expected [*is not* information])?
	What is different about the *is* information compared to the *is not* information? Are there any relevant changes?
	How do these causes explain what we know about the problem? Which cause seems most likely?
	How could we verify that our most likely cause is actually the true cause of the deviation?
Complex situations or issues	What were or are the various concerns surrounding this particular issue or situation?
	How did or might the concerns of different stakeholders vary?
	Which concerns had or have the highest priority?
	What steps were or could be taken to address each concern?

use. Remember that we don't necessarily need to use each step of a given process; sometimes a single step or two is sufficient to meet our objectives.

Applying the Process: Eating Disorders Example

The teacher decides to use each of the four situation appraisal steps.

Prepare lesson. Each teacher has a format for lesson plans that works well for that teacher. From our standpoint, the lesson's format is not important. We would, however, encourage each teacher, to consider the following questions in planning the lesson:

• Where specifically in the curriculum do you want to use the analytic process?
• What are you trying to accomplish?
• What do you want the students to know or be able to do as a result of this lesson?
• What process and how much of it do you want to introduce?
• How do you want the group structured—full class, small groups, pairs, or individuals?
• What instructional materials do you want to provide? Consider any additional content the students will need to answer the process questions.
• What additional materials will the students and you need? For example, do you want them to write on easel sheets, notepaper, or a blackboard? Do they need markers, chalk, pens, or other writing instruments?

• How will you introduce the process? Do you want to teach the process steps or simply ask the process questions? At first, you may want to try asking the process questions in everyday language. Such rephrasing can help you get more comfortable with the processes and immediately involve the students in considering each question.
• What questions are you going to ask students? What are you going to ask them to do? Consider the instructions you will give, the process questions you will ask them, and what you want them to do with the answer (e.g., write them down or answer orally).
• What is the estimated length of time you will spend on this lesson and each part of it?
• How will you measure success?

Applying the Process: Eating Disorders Example

The health teacher uses the preceding questions to develop a lesson plan, shown in Figure 7.6 (p. 124).

Teach lesson. We follow the lesson plan we developed, making notes as we go along.

Applying the Process: Eating Disorders Example

The teacher follows the key steps she identified in her plan and asks the process questions. As students work in small groups, they think about and record their answers. Each small group then presents their work to the whole class.

FIGURE 7.6
Health Teacher's Lesson Plan in the Eating Disorders Example

Lesson Objective	Materials Needed	Group Structure	Estimated Duration	Key Steps and Process Questions	Measures of Success
Students apply what they have learned about eating disorders (especially anorexia) to a real-life situation. Students use the situation appraisal process.	Newspaper article on eating disorders. Flip charts. Markers.	Small groups.	One class period.	Get students organized into small groups and assign roles. Have students read the article. *Ask:* If you were a friend of the girl in the article, what would you be concerned or worried about? List answers on paper. *Ask:* What do you mean by each one of those things you listed? Why is that a concern to you? Write an explanation next to each item. *Ask:* Although each of the concerns you listed needs to be addressed, which are most important? Put an asterisk next to the highest-priority concerns. *Ask:* What could you do to help the girl if you were her friend? What would be your next steps? Ask each group to present their work to the full class.	The extent to which they incorporate what they have learned about anorexia—the problems it can cause, the psychological profile of its sufferers, and the best way to approach it. How well they use the situation appraisal process. Even though it's the first time they use it, look for how well they answer the questions, organize, and address the information.

Assess results. During and after we complete the lesson, we consider the following questions:

- What are the lessons learned? What went particularly well? What could have gone better?
- What would we do differently next time? How can we make the lesson even more successful next time?

Applying the Process: Eating Disorders Example

As the health teacher considers the questions to assess results, she writes down these observations for next time:

- I was really pleased with how well the students used what they had learned about anorexia. They recognized its danger signs and areas of concern.
- The process flowed really smoothly. One area to spend more time on is setting priorities. The students want every issue to be high priority. Maybe next time I'll just have them pick the top five issues or concerns.
- A couple of students approached me after class and said they were worried about one of their friends; we talked about what they could do.

As we stated at the beginning of this book, these analytic tools build upon our commonsense responses to problems and situations by providing a structure to resolve issues. Knowingly or not, all of us use at least some of the elements of these processes at least some of the time. We may read about these tools and say something such as, "I do that" and "I use this." And we do those things! Chances are, however, that we have not consistently used all the ideas and their elements as described.

When we try to more consciously apply these ideas, it is as if we have acquired a new skill or fine-tuned an existing one. It may feel a bit awkward at first, like an experienced tennis player learning to change the way to hold a tennis racket. It feels wrong. Tiger Woods, the preeminent golf pro, recently spent a year changing his golf swing, even as his ranking on the tour fell. It took him about a year to relearn and become comfortable with the new swing. Then he won the U.S. Open by the largest margin in history. Sometimes it takes some short-term discomfort to reap longer-term rewards.

We hope we have intrigued you so that you want to take that first step. We are confident these tools can make a difference in your professional and personal life and in the lives of your students. These tools help maximize our ability to deal with difficult issues. So many of life's situations require us to reach workable and meaningful conclusions by effectively accessing, organizing, and using information and appropriately involving others. In this age of incomprehensible technological growth, the human mind is still the most powerful computer we have.

Appendix A: Contributing Educators

We are grateful for the examples contributed by the following teachers and administrators that we used in this book. This book could not have been possible without them.

Teacher	District
Linda Anderson	School District of Philadelphia (PA)
Terra Anderson	Magnolia School District (CA)
Frances Dick	Ascension Parish Schools (LA)
Gretchen Ernsdorf	Laguna Beach Unified School District (CA)
Brenda Hall-Covert	School District of Philadelphia (PA)
Lynne Harkness	Princeton Regional School District (NJ)
Mike Hyland	Montgomery Township Public Schools (NJ)
Ginny Klestinski	Wauwatosa School District (WI)
Carrie Leventhal	Laguna Beach Unified School District (CA)
Jan Manning	Brighton Area Schools (MI)
Mike McGuire	Laguna Beach Unified School District (CA)
Lynn Mederos	Orange County Public Schools (FL)
Rick Miller	Princeton Regional School District (NJ)
Tom Purdy	Laguna Beach Unified School District (CA)
Allison Ramus	Princeton Regional School District (NJ)
Emily Rice	Alexandria City Schools (VA)
Mike Roche	Laguna Beach Unified School District (CA)
Beth Smith	Phillipsburg Public Schools (NJ)
Paul Thusius	Wauwatosa School District (WI)
Sandy Wozniak	Mt. Olive Township Public Schools (NJ)
Peg Zwicki	Phillipsburg Public Schools (NJ)

Administrator	District
Anita Bacala	Ascension Parish Schools (LA)
Kathy Blackburn	Orange County Public Schools (FL)
David Collins	Orange County Public Schools (FL)
Sheila Fletcher	Lafourche Parish Schools (LA)
Debra Jones	Terrebonne Parish Schools (LA)
Jeff Keranen	Wauwatosa School District (WI)
Linda King	St. John Parish Schools (LA)
Bob Klempen	Orange County Public Schools (FL)
Anita Landry	Terrebonne Parish Schools (LA)
Debbie Manuel	Orange County Public Schools (FL)
Bonnie Riutta	Brighton Area Schools (MI)
Wayne Verdick	Terrebonne Parish Schools (LA)

We are indebted to teachers and administrators from the following districts whose examples we did not include but from whom we have learned a great deal:

Columbus City Schools (OH)
Corning-Painted Post Area School District (NY)
Dayton City Schools (OH)
Duval County Unified Schools (FL)
Greenwich Township School District (NJ)
Hackettstown Public Schools (NJ)
Livingston Public Schools (NJ)
Marysville E.V. Schools (OH)
North Warren Regional Schools (NJ)
Orrville City Schools (OH)
Placentia-Yorba Linda Unified School District (CA)
South Brunswick Public Schools (NJ)
Taylor School District (MI)
Warren County Vo-Tech Schools (NJ)
Warren Hills Regional High School District (NJ)

Appendix B: CompassQuest: Middle School/Corporate Project

In September 1998, the Tregoe Education Forum cosponsored—with the nation's leading curriculum-development organization, the Association for Supervision and Curriculum Development (ASCD)—a unique, three-year project to develop an alliance between a number of Kepner-Tregoe, Inc., clients and their local middle schools, grades 6 to 8.

The key objective of the CompassQuest consortium is to improve the way students, individually and in teams, ask questions and analyze information for problem solving and decision making. They learn to work effectively in teams, using a common language for solving problems and making decisions. And they learn to substantiate their conclusions.

The most important contribution those companies participating in the CompassQuest effort have made to the project is to share their brainpower. Kepner-Tregoe clients provide local schools with their expert problem solvers and decision makers, trained by Kepner-Tregoe. These experts have had years of experience developing critical-thinking skills within their organizations.

In each year of this project, the school teams and their corporate representatives have developed curriculum materials for teaching problem-solving and decision-making concepts to students and plans for applying these concepts to school operations. The model lessons and best practices that have emerged from this effort are shared with team members from other CompassQuest schools at two national meetings each year.

The middle schools and corporate partners listed below are all participants in the CompassQuest consortium:

Middle School	City and State	Corporate Partner
Chester M. Stevens Mt. Olive Middle School	Budd Lake, NJ	BASF
George Washington Middle School	Alexandria, VA	World Bank
Gonzales Middle School	Gonzales, LA	Uniroyal Chemical Co.
John Witherspoon Middle School	Princeton, NJ	Kepner-Tregoe, Inc.
Maitland Middle School	Maitland, FL	Tregoe Education Forum
Marysville E.V. School	Marysville, OH	Honda of America
Montgomery Middle School	Skillman, NJ	Johnson and Johnson
Painted Post Area School	Painted Post, NY	Corning, Inc.
Scranton Middle School	Brighton, MI	University of Michigan
Southmoor Middle School	Columbus, OH	Abbott Labs
Whitman Middle School	Wauwatosa, WI	Briggs and Stratton

Bibliography

Bateman, W. L. (1990). *Open to question*. San Francisco: Jossey-Bass.

Browne, M. N., & Keeley, S. M. (1994). *Asking the right questions*. Upper Saddle River, NJ: Prentice-Hall.

Bruner, J. S. (1973). *The relevance of education*. New York: W. W. Norton.

Christenbury, L., & Kelly, P. P. (1983). *Questioning: A path to critical thinking*. Urbana, IL: ERIC Clearinghouse on Reading and Communication Skills and the National Council of Teachers of English.

Dantonio, M. (1990). *How can we create thinkers?* Bloomington, IN: National Education Service.

Dorner, D. (1996). *The logic of failure*. Reading, MA: Metropolitan Books (Perseus Books).

Hunkins, F. P. (1995). *Teaching thinking through effective questioning* (2nd ed.). Norwood, MA: Christopher-Gordon Publishers.

Hyman, R. T. (1979). *Strategic questioning*. Englewood Cliffs, NJ: Prentice-Hall.

Kepner, C. H., & Tregoe, B. B. (1997). *The new rational manager: An updated edition for a new world*. Princeton, NJ: Kepner-Tregoe.

Leeds, D. (1987). *Smart questions: A new strategy for successful managers*. New York: McGraw-Hill.

Pasch, M., Langer, G., Gardner, T., Starko, A., & Moody, C. (1995). *Teaching as decision making*. New York: Longman Publishers.

Short, K., et al. (1996). *Learning together through inquiry*. York, ME: Stenhouse Publishers.

References

Avi. (1991). *Nothing but the truth: A documentary novel*. New York: Orchard Books.

Berryman, S., & Bailey, T. (1992). *The double helix of education and the economy*. New York: Institute of Education and the Economy, Teachers College/Columbia University.

Beyer, B. (1984, March). Improving thinking skills—Defining the problem. *Phi Delta Kappan, 67*(7), 486–490.

Beyer, B. (1987). *Practical strategies for the teaching of thinking*. Boston: Allyn and Bacon.

Bloomberg, M. (1997). *Bloomberg by Bloomberg*. New York: John Wiley & Sons.

Bourgeois, P. (1995). *Franklin wants a pet* (B. Clark, Illus.). New York: Scholastic.

Bromley, K. D. (1992). *Language arts: Exploring connections* (2nd ed.). Boston: Allyn and Bacon.

Cecil, N. L. (1995). *The art of inquiry*. Winnipeg, Canada: Peguis Publishers.

Costa, A. L. (Ed.). (1991). *Developing minds: A resource book for teaching thinking* (Rev. ed., Vol. 1). Alexandria, VA: Association for Supervision and Curriculum Development.

Dillon, J. T. (1990). *The practice of questioning*. London: Routledge.

Eales-White, R. (1998). *Ask the right question!* New York: McGraw-Hill.

Goodlad, J. I. (1984). *A place called school*. New York: McGraw-Hill.

Healy, J. M. (1990). *Endangered minds: Why our children don't think*. New York: Touchstone.

Johnson, N. L. (1992). *Thinking is the key*. Beavercreek, OH: Creative Learning Consultants.

Kepner, C. H., & Tregoe, B. B. (1965). *The rational manager*. Princeton, NJ: Kepner-Tregoe.

King, P. M., & Kitchener, K. S. (1994). *Developing reflective judgment*. San Francisco: Jossey-Bass.

Kyzer, S. P. (1996, November 21). Sharpening your critical-thinking skills—Professional development initiative. *Orthopedic Nursing, 15*(6), 66–74.

Langer, E. J. (1997). *The power of mindful learning*. New York: Addison-Wesley.

Miles, B. (1980). *Maudie and me and the dirty book*. New York: Knopf.

Myers, C. (1986). *Teaching students to think critically*. San Francisco: Jossey-Bass.

Olson, S. (1999, May/June). Candid camera. *Teacher Magazine, 10*(8), 29–32.

Paul, R. (1990). *Critical thinking: What every person needs to survive in a rapidly changing world*. Rohnert Park, CA: Center for Critical Thinking and Moral Critique, Sonoma State University.

Perkins, D. N. (1981). *The mind's best work*. Cambridge, MA: Harvard University Press.

Postman, N., & Weingarten, C. (1969). *Teaching as a subversive activity*. New York: Delacorte Press.

Richetti, C., & Sheerin, J. (1999, November). Helping students ask the right questions. *Educational Leadership, 57*(3), 58–62.

Ricks, D. (1993). *Blunders in international business*. Cambridge, MA: Blackwell.

Roden, C. V. (Ed.). (1987). *20/20 Business Thinking*. York, PA: Wellspring.

Rubenstein, R. (1998, March 18). Invest in brains. *Electronics Weekly*, 17–18.

Schank, R. C. (1991). *The connoisseur's guide to the mind*. New York: Summit Books.

Sternberg, R. J. (1996). *Successful intelligence*. New York: Simon & Schuster.

Stigler, J. W., & Hiebert, J. (1999). *The teaching gap*. New York: The Free Press.

Vroom, V. H., & Yetton, W. P. (1973). *Leadership and decision making*. Pittsburgh: University of Pittsburgh Press.

Wales, C., Nardi, A., & Stager, R. (1986, May). Decision making: A new paradigm for education. *Educational Leadership, 43*(8), 37–41.

Wilen, W. W. (1991). *Questioning skills for teachers* (3rd ed.). Washington, DC: National Education Association.

Index

Note: An *f* after a page number indicates a reference to a figure.

About the Authors

Cynthia T. Richetti is Vice President of the Tregoe Education Forum. She works with teachers and administrators from elementary, middle, and high schools in urban, rural, and suburban districts in the development and implementation of critical-thinking skills projects. Her areas of expertise include instructional materials development, adult learning, results measurement, culture change, and team building.

Before joining the Tregoe Education Forum in 1994, Richetti was a consultant with Kepner-Tregoe, Inc., an international management consulting firm. During her nine years with Kepner-Tregoe, she held positions in product and consultant development and support and worked with clients on consulting assignments.

Richetti holds a B.A. degree from Colgate University and M.S. degree in organizational dynamics from the University of Pennsylvania. She is coauthor with James Sheerin of "Helping Students Ask the Right Questions" (*Educational Leadership*, November 1999).

Benjamin B. Tregoe is founder and Chair of the Tregoe Education Forum. He has more than 40 years' experience in improving critical thinking in industry and government. In 1958, after working as a research scientist at the RAND Corporation, he cofounded Kepner-Tregoe, Inc., a Princeton-based, international management consulting firm. In 1993, he founded the Tregoe Education Forum as a nonprofit organization to bring these same critical-thinking skills to elementary, middle, and high school students and school administrators.

Tregoe is a leading lecturer and has published extensively throughout the world. Millions of managers worldwide have read *The Rational Manager*, a landmark book in the field of management methodology, which Tregoe coauthored with Charles Kepner. It was revised in 1981 and again in 1997, as *The New Rational Manager: An Updated Edition for a New World*. He has also coauthored *Top Management Strategy: What It Is and How To Make It Work*, with John W. Zimmerman, and *Vision in Action: Putting a Winning Strategy to Work*, with colleagues Ronald A. Smith, Peter M. Tobia, and John W. Zimmerman. His latest book, *The Culture of Success: Building a Sustained Competitive Advantage by*

Living Your Corporate Beliefs, was written with John W. Zimmerman.

Tregoe holds a Ph.D. from Harvard University, where he has served as chair of an advisory council to the dean of the graduate school of arts and sciences. He has served on the boards of a number of educational and business organ-izations and is a member of the Human Resource Development Hall of Fame.

Both authors can be reached at Tregoe Education Forum, P.O. Box 289, Research Rd., Princeton, NJ 08542; phone: 609-252-2581; fax: 609-921-7624; e-mail: crichetti@tregoe.org.

Related ASCD Resources: Effective Leadership

Analytic Processes for School Leaders: An ASCD Action Tool shows how to apply the theory explained in the book. This action tool has two components: a handbook and a videotape. The *Analytic Processes for School Leaders Handbook* provides exercises for applying the four rational-thinking processes in K–12 classroom and administrative situations. Readers are taken step by step through each process. The videotape, *Analytic Processes for School Leaders: Scenarios*, illustrates key elements of the processes in a variety of classroom settings. #701016

ASCD stock numbers are not...

Audiotapes

Action Research: Easy Steps to Prog... Assessment by Jeffery Glanz (#

On Action Research by Carl Glickma...

*Data Driven Decision-Making: Changin... Instruction to Improve Student Outc... Rutlin, Mark Shibles, and Michael ... (#200197)

Decision Making Matrix: Who Decides What: Ness (#299328)

*Intuitive Leadership: A Principal's Plan for Actio... Jacqueline Carothers and Karen Dyer (#2...

Strategic Leadership: Implementing New Paradigm... Learning, Education, and Reform by Charles Schwahn and William Spady (#200083)

*A Systems Approach to Standards-Based Education Au... from the 2000 Teaching and Learning Conference b... Carolee Hayes and Jane Ellison (#200315)

Online Professional Development

ASCD Professional Development Online Courses (available at http://www.ascd.org/framepdonline.html): Effective Leadership, Systems Thinking, and Problem Solving and Decision Making

Print Products

Guiding School Improvement with Action Research by Richard Sagor (#100047)

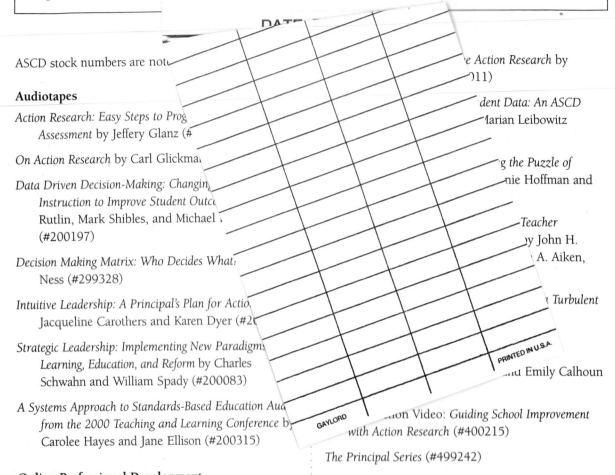

...*e Action Research* by ...011)

...*dent Data: An ASCD* ...Marian Leibowitz

...*g the Puzzle of* ...nie Hoffman and

...*Teacher* ...y John H. ...A. Aiken,

...*Turbulent*

...and Emily Calhoun

...ion Video: *Guiding School Improvement with Action Research* (#400215)

The Principal Series (#499242)

Shared Decision Making Series by Cynthia Harrison, Al Shanker, and John Goodlad (#614253)

For more information, visit us on the World Wide Web (http://www.ascd.org); send an e-mail message to member@ascd.org; call the ASCD Service Center (1-800-933-ASCD or 703-578-9600, then press 2); send a fax to 703-575-5400; or write to Information Services, ASCD, 1703 N. Beauregard St., Alexandria, VA 22311-1714 USA.